THE SHAKEOUTS OF

ROCK & ROLL

by

Freddie Downs

Imprint Edition: Create Space, Scotts Valley, CA

ISBN 13: 978-1515075493
ISBN 10: 1515075494

- What and when were the five shakeouts of Rock & Roll?
- The reason The Rock and Roll Hall of Fame is located in Cleveland?
- The only hit to top the Pop, Soul and Country Charts simultaneously?
- The reason the five original MTV veejays left the network in1986?
- The first mass-released stereo single? The first cassette single?

It's all here in "The Five Shakeouts of Rock & Roll" along with a chart contrasting the rock era to the pre-rock era, the top ten that never were, rock & roll Christmas, ten one-hit wonders that made a difference and much more.

This book takes you back to the early obscure beginnings of the music and brings you right up to today. In between, you'll trace the origin of the sports anthem, important songwriters, concert moments that hang in history, video landmarks, times of triumph and tragedy. The music was always there and now you can be there, too.

Thirty years and ten constructions in the making, "The Five Shakeouts of Rock & Roll" is written by former Kansas City area radio announcer Freddie Downs (KUDL, KCLO) and author of "Rock & Roll Then and Now", "Life Rocks" and "Radio Rocks" (2003, Waltsan Publishing). If you love this music, treat yourself to a book that loves it, too—one of the few books that doesn't say 'my generation was cooler than yours'. Each generation made an important contribution to this sixty+year musical "fad" that spans the baby boomers to Generation Now. "The Five Shakeouts of Rock & Roll" will leave you waiting for the next five and give you a good read while you wait.

DEDICATION

In 1981, a package containing this manuscript and the only copies of all of the photos broke open while passing through the automated equipment at a New York City Post Office, dealing a potentially fatal blow to this project.

For nearly five months, the contents were lost with little hope of returning to the author. Then, an alert postal service employee at the loose-in-the-mail warehouse just doing his/her job somehow uncovered the manuscript and every one of the photos and returned them in excellent condition.

Although I will never know the name of the person who brought this book back from the brink of disaster, he/she has my heartfelt thanks and eternal gratitude. Whoever you are…this book is dedicated to you.

FOREWARD

DEFINING SHAKEOUTS

A shakeout is a moment in music history when the old way of doing business doesn't work anymore, the icons drop by the wayside and new artists and styles fill the void. The audience also might be totally new, depending on how jarring the changes are to an individual's comfort zone.

Music never remains static, but rock & roll always tries to have it both ways, disconnecting from its past while only one retro fad away from undoing the divorce. There is a thread between Wynonie Harris belting his heart out in 1948 and Usher at the top of his vocal game today, of Lesley Gore's 1963 teen angst and Britney Spears dancing in the same high school hallways in 1998, of Alanis Morrissette in 1996 and Adele in 2011 both finding their initial fame with angry songs about ex-boyfriends who 'did them wrong'.

Each generation forges the same conceit that they alone invented the world two weeks ago and anything prior to that has no correlation to the present. That tunnel vision is a license for youth only to find true balance when some dinosaur rock band lets rip with a riff that was only recognized as something from recent times.

The rock star today is laying the groundwork for whatever will follow when you have kids. These shakeouts are important because they provide new blood, and new direction. And if you hang with it, you can be young not just once, but possibly for a lifetime.

…Freddie Downs

BEFORE THE ROCK ERA   THE ROCK ERA

BEFORE THE ROCK ERA	THE ROCK ERA
Jazz and classical morphed in George Gershwin's "Rhapsody in Blue".	Rock and opera morphed in "Bohemian Rhapsody" by Queen.
Accurate sales figures were not kept on artists like Bing Crosby and Billy Murray. Both had long careers and possibly exceeded Elvis Presley in sales.	During 1980, Elvis Presley sold his one billionth record, the highest recorded sales in music history.
Bobby soxers screamed and swooned for Frank Sinatra in the 1940's.	Groupies do everything a rock star asks.
During World Wars I and II, it would have been unpatriotic not to support your country at war. Songs were almost unanimously pro-war – "Over There", "We Did It Before and We Can Do It Again".	Since the 1960's, music has questioned the wisdom of war and those who wage it – "Where Have All the Flowers Gone," "99 Luftballoons".
Billie Holiday's 1946 R&B hit "Strange Fruit" focused on white lynch mobs. Otherwise, the issue of race was avoided.	Rap acts focus on every aspect of life in the black community.

The Charlston, the Jitterbug, the Limbo.	The Twist, the Hustle, the Macarena.
Glenn Miller's plane vanishes over the English Channel. He was presumably killed by an Allied plane discarding its unused bombs.	John Lennon is assassinated by a disturbed fan.
The phonograph is invented in 1877, cylinders and 78 rpm records, radio, the microphone, the electric guitar.	Television, magnetic recording tape which makes stereo possible, the 33 1/3 rpm album, the 45 rpm single, cassettes, VHS, cable TV, CDs, DVDs, satellite radio.
Irving Berlin, Cole Porter, Tin Pan Alley.	Jerry Leiber & Mike Stoller, Carole King & Gerry Goffin, The Brill Building.

"Tumbling Tumbleweeds". "San Antonio Rose". "Wabash Cannon Ball". Songs of trains, cowboys and cattle drives put the western in country western music.	Outlaw country takes root in 1955 with "Sixteen Tons" and "Folsom Prison Blues". You either "owe your soul to the company stove", "you shot a man in Reno just to watch him die" or some other grim reality.
Guy Lombardo ushers in the New Year from the Waldorf Astoria Hotel in New York with his signature "Auld Lang Syne".	Dick Clark's "New Year's Rockin' Eve" from Times Square.
The radio show "Your Hit Parade" counts down the hits.	"American Top 40" with Casey Kasem.
V-J Day, August, 1945. Wild partying in the streets and an all star radio concert that night to celebrate the end of World War II.	Woodstock: August, 1969. The youth culture takes a weekend off from Vietnam for an oasis of music and social harmony.
The Stork Club, The Cocoanut Grove and during World War II, The Hollywood Canteen and The Stage Door Canteen.	The 60s: The Whiskey A Go Go and The Fillmores West and East. The 70s: Studio 54. Since the 70s: CBGBs.

Bandleader Ozzie Nelson and vocalist Harriet Hilliard, stars of the big band era.	Their son, Rick Nelson and his sons Matthew and Gunnar, rock stars of the 50s/60s and 90s.
Adults shaped the world.	It's a youth culture!
An album was a collection of 78 rpm shellac records. Singles were 78s.	First singles vanish in the 90s. Then major record retailers like Tower Records close shop in the 21st century. The album could be the next fatality as consumers anoint the hits through Internet downloads, leaving behind the music they don't want.

SHAKEOUT #1

FROM RACE MUSIC TO RHYTHM

& BLUES TO ROCK & ROLL

1948-1954

If you were white you missed it. During the 1940s, small independent record labels specializing in music by black artists decided that the best way to increase sales was to sponsor late night radio programs featuring the music. While white America slept, the shows popped up in every major city attempting to target the music to the black audience. Then in 1948, "race music" collided with the future when Wynonie "Blues" Harris' hit "Good Rockin' Tonight" put all the pieces together for what would later be known as rock & roll. That same year, WDIA, Memphis became the first radio station in the world to feature a black music format 24 hours a day.

What followed during the next six years were innovations including the 33 1/3 rpm long play album and 45 rpm single (ending the reign of the 78 rpm single, the standard music for fifty years), recording tape which vetted stereo, and the rise of television's popularity at radio's expense which led to music formats like Top Forty that opened the culture to music no longer restrained by racial barriers.

During this period, white college students and adults unknowingly purchased the music causing selected songs to crossover to pop stations and the Billboard Pop Chart. The racial climate in America kept the music contained for as long as possible. The period would remain cloaked in obscurity for decades with the pioneers of rock & roll never receiving the credit due them. But the seeds for all that followed started here.

1948

Fragments of the style that would eventually be known as rock & roll could be heard in a variety of blues, boogie woogie, country swing and jump jazz records dating from the 1920s. But the artist who first put all of the elements together was Wynonie "Blues" Harris on December 28, 1947 in Cincinnati, Ohio when he recorded "Good Rockin' Tonight" for the King label.

Released during February, 1948, it sold a phenomenal 500,000 copies in its first five days, reaching #1 on Billboard's Race Music Chart and going on to become the second biggest R&B record for the year. With this performance, Harris invented the prototype for all rock & roll acts that followed. The song was anchored in a distinct beat. Harris' hoarse suggestive vocal gave the song an air of sexuality and danger while his bump and grind stage routine would serve as a blueprint for later acts like Elvis Presley to drive women into a sexual frenzy.

When "Good Rockin' Tonight" was originally recorded by Roy Brown in 1947, it was just another peppy jazz hit not unlike a dozen other hits at the time. Wynonie Harris' vulgar audacity gave the song a new energy, attitude and beat while unknowingly predicting the future direction of popular music well beyond the confines of R&B.

Forces were gradually taking shape at this moment which would result in the eventual evolution of rock & roll. As Harris' "Good Rockin' Tonight" began its descent down the Chart, another R&B hit "We're Gonna Rock, We're Gonna Roll" (Wild Bill Moore) on the Savoy label debuted in June, eventually reaching #1 on the Race Music Chart with its mix of boogie woogie piano and sax honking in the lower register.

Neither song reached the ears of white America at the time, but both loomed large with the "fringe time" deejays who spun R&B records in the late hours while America slept. The music industry's greatest secret was that rhythm and blues music performed by black artists was selling hundreds of thousands to a black audience with no exposure from the white community, but even this was about to change.

During 1948, WDIA, Memphis became the first radio station in the country where a black staff played black music twenty-four hours a day. Among the WDIA deejays were two future singing stars—Riley "B.B". King and Rufus Thomas. Many of the "fringe time" deejays were white, like Hunter Hancock who had been playing R&B in Los Angeles since 1942. On June 14, 1948 KFVD, Los Angeles made the bold move of bringing Hancock's "Harlem Matinee" to afternoons six days a week. Whenever the black music made the daylight hours, it was initially received with indignation or ignored by whites while blacks viewed it as one of the equalizing factors for their imperfect world.

Parallel to the developments in the black community were events in the white world which were already in flux. The big band era had died a natural death leaving pop music to the throes of ballad singers and novelty records. The postwar baby boom officially began on January 1, 1946, and these children of the World War II generation would be searching for their own identity and a music separate from that of their parents.

The recording industry itself was undergoing great change. On June 21, 1948, Columbia Records introduced the 33 1/3 rpm microgroove record redefining the record album as a single long playing disc with ten to twelve songs instead of a package comprised of five or six 78s. Hello vinyl, goodbye shellac. A quieter revolution took place during August, 1948 when Capitol Records became the first record company to use magnetic recording tape, opening the door to stereo and other multi-tracking capabilities.

Within the music industry debates erupted over the frenetic sax wailing of Illinois Jacquet and pioneering use of the electric guitar by Les Paul and T Bone Walker. Was it simply noise or a new progression?

Net work radio shows like "Jack Benny" and "Suspense" were still the reigning form of entertainment, but NBC was pioneering the new medium of television with *Howdy Doody, Milton Berle and Kukla, Fran & Ollie*. America would quickly become addicted to the visual image leaving radio a void to fill if it was to continue to survive.

That void, along with the swift current of social change causing so much of the status quo to melt away, would mean that blacks and whites would no longer be able to live in totally separate worlds. A form of music hardly noticed in 1948 was about to create the bridge.

1949

At KOWH, Omaha, a station owned by Todd Storz, the Top Forty format debuted in 1949. After observing the way that teenagers played the same songs in repetition on a juke box, Storz fashioned the radio format which featured a tight playlist and limited deejay patter.

Research of local record sales determined the playlist. The idea was deceptively simple—play only the most popular music and everyone will listen. In the effort to provide a mainstream overview of pop, county, jazz and other forms of music, Top Forty would eventually serve as an unwitting catalyst in the evolution of rock & roll music, introducing black music into the pop culture on a scale that had never before been witnessed. Other Storz stations including WHB, Kansas City, KOMA, Oklahoma City and WTIX, New Orleans adapted the format, as well as those from competing radio chains owned by Gordon McLendon and Gerald Bartell.

Top Forty was as much a rigid formula as R&B was the music of spontaneity and gut feeling, seemingly worlds apart. No better example arose in 1949 than "Drinkin' Wine Spo-Dee-O-Dee" (Stick McGhee & His Buddies), a jubilant celebration of all night drinking binges with no sweetening for the general audience. Originally recorded in 1946 for the tiny Gotham label, the song was given up for dead when Ahmet Ertegun used a spirited second version to launch his influential Atlantic label during March, 1949.

The year also witnessed a major dance craze with "The Hucklebuck" (Paul Williams), a song covered by several R&B acts and alluded to in other R&B hits like "All She Wants To Do Is Rock" (Wynonie "Blues" Harris) and "Rock The Joint" (Jimmy Preston).

Since a popular dance craze is the worst kept secret, the Hucklebuck quickly flared in popularity among whites. The filtering system that kept those "gutter voices" and "sax honkers" off the pop stations suddenly found the dance socially acceptable in white pop versions by Tommy Dorsey and Frank Sinatra, a preview of the double standard that would rule for a decade.

To whites, Perry Como was the biggest pop star in 1949 with 17 Chart hits that year. Nearly every neighborhood had at least one TV where people would congregate. And during March, 1949, RCA Victor introduced the 45 rpm single, a step forward in sound quality that required a plastic adapter to compensate for its wide hole when played on existing phonographs. The 78 rpm record, the standard for a half century, seemed doomed.

On the black side of town, the sequels kept appearing like "Rock the House" (Tiny Grimes) and "Rock and Roll" (Wild Bill Moore). Early strains of doo-wop street corner harmony were evident in "What Are You Doing New Year's Eve?" (The Orioles) while Johnny Otis, a white musician who lived the life of a black, paid tribute to Los Angeles disc jockey Hunter Hancock with his song "Head Hunter".

History was made again at WDIA, Memphis with the

introduction of the rock era's first female disc jockey, Martha Jean "The Queen" Steinberg. Her impact would span several decades and cities including serving as a voice of reason in Detroit during the 1960s to quell race riots.

Rhythm and blues was now a driving force in the black community, but rock & roll was still looked upon as a musical spasm no more significant than mambo records. Even Wynonie Harris expressed his frustration about being offered so many rock songs. At this point, neither whites nor blacks understood what had been let loose upon the land.

1950

An accident at a bedspring factory where he worked crushed his hands and doctors were discussing amputation, but Antoine "Fats" Domino underwent rigorous physical therapy for a full recovery. Months later, the 19-year-old Domino recorded "The Fat Man" with its 'life-I-love-you' attitude and a message of just because a man weighs 200+ pounds doesn't mean he can't be a hit with women, lead an active life and enjoy a normal level of happiness.

While it didn't signal a trend for overweight chic, it did humanize the situation while giving overweight people their own party anthem. "The Fat Man" barreled onto the R&B Chart during January, 1950, becoming the biggest R&B hit of the year. By mid-1951, it had sold a million copies, the first hit for both Fats and his label Imperial Records. Domino would go on to sell 65 million records, becoming the top act for the decade on the Billboard R&B Chart.

Unlike other acts that would trade on an image of sex or outrageousness, Fats simply came across as a warm, smiling human being, although many of his lyrics were bitter or morose, practically in contrast to the man performing them. His unique vocal style with a French/Creole inflection and his flattop hairdo provided much of his image, yet his most enduring legacy was the New Orleans sound which combined elements of jazz with R&B to remain relevant well into the 70s with a succession of acts that included professor Longhair, Lloyd Price, Clarence "Frogman" Henry, Huey "Piano" Smith, Frankie Ford, Lee Dorsey, Ernie K-Doe, The Dixie Cups, Aaron Neville and Dr. John.

Fats patterned his piano style after R&B innovator Amos Milburn whose 1947 hit "Chickenshack Boogie" proved to be an important transitional hit to rock & roll. On September 21, 1950 in Los Angeles, Milburn recorded an obscure 1936 pop tune "Glory of Love" which would become the decade's foremost ballad of undying love in a series of subsequent versions by The Five Keys, The Velvetones and The Roommates.

Another early R&B innovator, Roy Brown, author of "Good Rockin' Tonight", showed ever greater intuition with the release of "Teenage Jamboree" during December, 1950. Instead of utilizing the usual R&B themes of booze, fast cars and sex, this hit centered around a teenage dance party where the pleasures were music, hot dogs and soda pop. It was still several years before the emergence of the youth culture, yet "Teenage Jamboree" signaled the direction in which the music would eventually turn.

1951

With a number of R&B hits selling a million copies or more, it was only a matter of time before one would finally break through to the Billboard Pop Chart. For this to happen, pop stations would have to play it and whites would have to purchase it. Even though whites usually preferred safe, pleasant pop music like Nat King Cole if they tolerated black voices at all, a white groundswell brought one of the least likely candidates – a song about sex – to the historic designation as the first black rock & roll hit to crossover to the Billboard Pop Chart.

"Sixty Minute Man" (The Dominoes) told the whimsical story of Old Dan who extends the invitation to fill in for all husbands and boyfriends not measuring up to their sexual potential. Not that sex was directly mentioned, merely alluded to in the chorus "rock 'em, roll 'em all night long".

White college students were quick to champion the song, but it was soon their parents who fueled the breakthrough. Some might have misread the sexual overtones, while others corrupted the idea into a racial stereotype too boastful to be true. Most likely the moral climate was greatly exaggerated, and millions of white adults who were socially circumspect held a clandestine longing to be Old Dan just to experience what it would be like to outlast any number of women for an hour at a time.

Whatever it said about white society, "Sixty Minute Man" became that one R&B record that was permissible to enjoy. During August, 1951, it crossed over to the Billboard Pop Chart where it remained for 23 weeks. For forty years the single remained the biggest hit in the history of the Soul Chart, spending 30 weeks in the R&B top ten, 12 of those at #1! For all that it achieved, it segued to oblivion. Whites immediately turned their attention back to dancing the mambo and loving Lucy on TV, no more inclined to buy black music than they were before. The Dominoes wouldn't return to the Pop Chart until 1957.

Parallel to the popularity of "Sixty Minute Man", another giant hit, "Rocket 88" by Jackie Brenston & His Delta Cats (actually the Ike Turner Band), made a quick dash to #1 R&B. Originally cut at The Memphis Recording Service which later became Sun Records, the song was leased to the Chicago-based Chess label. "Rocket 88" paid tribute to the sleek Oldsmobile with the V-8 engine and a night of "boozin' and cruisin'", its over-amped bass and frenetic sax wailing setting it apart as thee year's prime example of rock & roll.

This distinction wasn't lost on Dave Miller, the owner of Holiday/Essex Records in Philadelphia who decided that the time was right for a white cover version of the song. Although they were at first hesitant to record a song that represented a departure from their country western style, Bill Haley & The Saddlemen obliged their employer. The experiment wasn't altogether successful, but in Miller's mind it wasn't over yet.

Like Miller, other white business owners were testing the waters of the burgeoning R&B movement. Leo Mintz, the owner of Record Rendezvous in Cleveland, Ohio, purchased a three-hour block of time each evening at 11:15 on WJW to increase the sale of black music at his store.

Mintz's brainchild "Moondog House" debuted on July 11, 1951, quickly becoming the most important connection between black teenagers and the emerging R&B scene throughout Ohio and neighboring states. Its charismatic host, Alan Freed, would shift gears from his primetime classical music program to become a manic creature of rhythm in the after hours, howling like a dog and opening the mic during records to pound out a beat on a telephone directory or to interject his own call and response with the music. The audience could not have cared less that the deejay was white. The music was unadulterated R&B like "Flamingo" (Earl Bostic), "I Got Loaded" (Peppermint Harris), "Glory of Love" (The Five Keys) and "The Right String But the Wrong Yo Yo" (Piano Red).

Meanwhile, in Atlanta at a talent show hosted by disc jockey Zenas Sears, local sensation Little Richard was signed by RCA for modest hits like "Taxi Blues" and "Get Rich Quick", the meager beginnings for a career that would catch fire several labels later.

1952

"Moondog House" transformed R&B from the forbidden fruit of dangerous dives and adult juke joints to the vicarious thrill of black teenagers who listened clandestinely with ears pressed tightly against the electric radio as not to arouse the ire of slumbering parents.

While the adult world slept, black teenagers discovered the music of Joe Turner, Wynonie Harris, Fats Domino, Amos Milburn, The Orioles and many other acts that were once the exclusive province of black club denizens. The radio itself became the summit and Alan Freed the un-anointed keeper of the beat.

With his radio program so widely successful, Freed sought to take it to the next level with a concert featuring the recording acts popular with his audience and in doing so crown himself the king of the black youth culture which he had helped to create.

"The Moondog Coronation Ball" was scheduled to take place at the Cleveland Arena from 10:00 p.m. – 2:00 a.m. on Friday, March 21 featuring Paul Williams, Tiny Grimes, The Dominoes and Varetta Dillard. After months of promotion pushing the anticipation level past all expectations, the concert sold out.

Thousands of black teenagers streamed into Cleveland not just from nearby cities but adjoining states! The word had spread that this was the only place to be, the seminal event of a lifetime, and the masses came to experience the music, to meet The Moondog, to be a part of history.

That evening as a light mist fell, a crowd of thousands formed on Euclid Avenue just outside the arena. Extending from one side of the street to the other and as far as the eye could see, the mass of humanity waited patiently, naïve to the events about to follow.

A little before 10:00 p.m. the steel doors of the arena were secured with a capacity crowd inside and may times that number stranded in the street. Sax man Paul Williams, the originator of the Hucklebuck, took the stage and began his set, the show being broadcast live that evening by WJW.

Once the music began the crowd outside surged forward buckling the steel doors. Even as every available inch of space disappeared, the crowd kept pressing forward, drawn to the music and the immediacy of the moment. Knives flashed, fights erupted, yet people kept dancing as the crowd pressed forward relentlessly.

During the third number, the fire marshal rang the curtain down. None of the other acts performed, most of them feeling fortunate to have escaped alive. Freed's entourage also made it through the melee with harrowing stories of women grinding their heels into anyone under foot and vandals trashing anything that wasn't nailed down. One stabbing was reported, but many more witnessed by those in attendance.

For a concert that didn't come off, the aftershocks would be felt for the next forty years. It was here that the music first drew a massive teenage audience which would give the event the distinction as the first rock & roll concert. The sheer numbers also proved the pulling power of radio. Instead of giving Freed a rebuke for causing a riot, WJW made the most of the situation with a flyer that proudly proclaimed: "Radio alone pulled 25,000!" TV had killed network radio, but music would be radio's salvation.

The audience didn't blame Freed for the fiasco. Like the music, he had taken a chance and those who attended usually spoke of it in positive terms. At year's end, The Treniers paid tribute to Freed with their R&B hit "The Moon Dog".

The Freed mythology of coining the phrase "rock & roll" and hosting the first rock & roll concert were the reasons that The Rock and Roll Hall of Fame was established in Cleveland in 1995. Taken in the long view, that $1.50 ticket to "The Moondog Coronation Ball" bought a lot more than just three songs from a sax player.

1952 was also the year that the Specialty label was launched with the year's top R&B hit "Lawdy Miss Clawdy" (Lloyd Price) featuring Fats Domino on the piano, the Atlantic label's second major hit "One Mint Julep" (The Clovers), "Night Train" (Jimmy Forrest), "Rock Rock Rock" (Amos Milburn) written by Peppermint Harris, "I'm Gonna Rock Some More" (Piano Red), Bill Haley & The Saddlemen's remake of the 1949 Jimmy Preston hit "Rock The Joint" and Clyde McPhatter doing some of his most impassioned vocal work with The Dominoes' up-tempo street corner harmony "That's What You're Doing To Me" and the eerie half-sung, half-wept reading of "The Bells" pertaining to a man viewing his own funeral from a higher vantage point.

During 1952, Bob Horn and Lee Stewart, two WFIL deejays, began hosting the locally televised "Philadelphia Bandstand" playing records and spotlighting teenagers dancing in the studio, an early hint of the youth culture about to take shape in white America.

1953

The age of the big momma arrived with Ruth Brown ("Mama He Treats Your Daughter Mean"), the gospel influenced Faye Adams ("Shake a Hand") and the year's top R&B hit by Willie Mae Thornton ("Hound Dog") rocking along with its self-assured intensity while serving advocacy to every woman who was ever 'done wrong' by her man.

In spite of the worldly voice growling the lyrics, "Hound Dog" was created by two white songwriters from New York City, Jerry Leiber and Mike Stoller, easily the most significant force in songwriting during the 1950s.

During April, Bill Haley and His Comets became the first white rock & roll act to make the Billboard Pop Chart with Haley's original composition "Crazy Man Crazy". The Orioles had an historic year with the solid R&B success "Hold Me Thrill Me Kiss Me" followed by "Crying in the Chapel" which became the second R&B hit to cross over to the Billboard Pop Chart (the first since "Sixty Minute Man" in 1951.

In Memphis, Sun Records was becoming a regional powerhouse in R&B with hits that included "Mystery Train" (Little Junior Parker) and "Bear Cat" (Rufus Thomas), an answer record to "Hound Dog". During June, Sun released the original version of the 50s standard "Just Walkin' In the Rain" by The Prisonaires, a vocal group consisting of five inmates from the Tennessee State Penitentiary. Pop star Johnny Ray sold more copies with his cover version, but couldn't match the simplicity of the original or the disarming vocal delivery of the Prisonaires' lead tenor Johnny Bragg.

1953 was the year The Dominoes fired Clyde McPhatter, replacing him with Jackie Wilson. Atlantic Records immediately structured a new group around McPhatter, The Drifters, whose debut hit "Money Money" became a rock classic.

On March 31, 1953, "Rock Around the Clock", written by Max C. Freedman and Jimmy DeKnight (real name: James Myers), was published by Myers Music. Weeks later the song was a hot regional hit in Delaware by Sonny Dae & His Knights, but Philadelphia-based Arcade label couldn't get the song to break anywhere else. For this song the third time would be the charm.

Throughout America events were gradually moving pop music in a new direction. In Los Angeles, record producer Buck Ram discovered the operatic voice of Tony Williams at a talent show hosted by disc jockey Hunter Hancock, the first step toward fashioning the vocal group The Platters. At the same time, 14-year-old Phil and his 16-year-old brother Don were touring the Midwest in their parents' country act, The Everly Family.

In Memphis, an 18-year-old truck driver, Elvis Presley, cut a private recording at the Memphis Recording Service, a business aligned with Sun Records, unaware that fame was only a year away. But the greatest drama took place in Cleveland where disc jockey Alan Freed suffered extensive facial injuries in an automobile accident. After plastic surgery, Freed returned bigger than ever, hitting the road with his "Biggest Rhythm and Blues Show" featuring Wynonie Harris, Joe Turner, Fats Domino and Ruth Brown. Even New York City had to take notice.

1954

It was the year that R&B came out of the fringe time closet. Pop stations including WHBQ, Memphis, WLAC, Nashville and KDAV, Lubbock, Texas featured the music during the afternoon/prime time hours. Deejays like Dewey Phillips, WHBQ (the first to air an Elvis Presley record), Bill "Hoss" Allen and John R. (John Richbourg) at WLAC and Douglas "Jocko" Henderson of WDAS/WOV Radio, New York City led the charge. Henderson brought his all star R&B reviews to the Apollo Theater while Atlanta deejay Zenas Sears purchased WATL, installing a 24-hour R&B format under the new call letters WOAK and syndicating his R&B program "Blues Caravan" to stations in Newark, New Jersey, Norfolk, Virginia and Chicago, Illinois, bringing the music to areas that might otherwise not hear it.

On September 8, 1954 Alan Freed helped to launch the new rock & roll format at WINS, New York, bringing with him a personal record library with thousands of songs. His program became the most influential, making an impact in concerts, recordings, movies and television. At year's end, Freed shared songwriting credit with Harvey Fuqua for "Sincerely" (The Moonglows).

All of this activity began to register nationally. As greater inroads were made to the white audience, a number of mainstream R&B hits received air play on pop stations, crossing over to the Billboard Pop Chart including "Gee" (The Crows), "Earth Angel" (The Penguins) and that breezy, wistful look at the 50s love "Sh-Boom" (The Chords).

Full scale acceptance of R&B was still wishful thinking since much of the white community took moral exception to the music. The year's top R&B hit "Shake Rattle and Roll" (Joe Turner) was more suggestive than most whites would tolerate. Even some black music programs chose to sidestep "Work With Me Annie" (The Midnighters) and "Honey Love" (The Drifters), sex hits that left little to the imagination. And a song like "Riot In Cell Block #9" (The Robins) written by Lieber & Stoller was unthinkable for a pop station, a prison song complete with the sound of sirens and machine gun volleys.

Most of the major record labels chose to ignore what was bubbling beneath the surface, but the Decca label compromised, hiring Bill Haley & The Comets, a white act from Essex, to record a cover version of the unsuccessful 1953 R&B single "(We're Gonna) Rock Around The Clock". Released during April, it was truly a record in search of a radio format. The vocal was too white and country to qualify for R&B yet the band's performance had too many flashes of jazz and R&B to work well in a country or pop formula. For the second time in two years, "Rock Around The Clock" came up empty.

Undeterred, Decca sent Haley back to the studio to rush a cover record of "Shake Rattle and Roll" which did well on the Pop Chart that summer as did the follow-up "Dim Dim The Lights". Many unsuspecting adults fueled Haley's early success, uncertain how to classify his music. Even Decca passed it off on the record label as "fox trot tempo", hardly the warning of a musical revolution.

In the ennui of white suburbia, no one had taken inventory of the large population of disaffected white youth. Some found a voice in R&B, others in Haley and many more in the year's top movie of non-conformity, "The Wild One", starring Marlon Brando. For different reasons, none of these factors united the factions.

Sam Phillips, the owner of Sun Records, thought that the answer would be a white artist who could sing black and his dream was realized on July 6, 1954 when 19-year-old Elvis Presley literally invented the Sun rock-a-billy sound with "That's All Right". It sold a respectable 20,000 copies in the south and its follow-up, a remake of "Good Rockin' Tonight" also did well. Elvis was burning up the south.

Even as new acts were finding their niche, the roots artists from the 1940s and early 50s noticed their services in less demand either due to their age or the perception that their musical style was outdated. Wynonie Harris, Amos Milburn, Roy Brown and The Orioles were among the acts to lose out in the first rock & roll shakeout. Johnny Ace ("Cross My Heart") had been another of the early icons.

On December 24, 1954 while trying to impress some women backstage at The Houston City Auditorium, the 26-year-old singer stuck a revolver to his head and pulled the trigger. The gun's only bullet fired and hours later Johnny Ace was dead. A week later, "Pledging My Love" became his first hit to reach the Pop Chart as the public searched its lyrics for any explanation of the tragedy which occurred at the junction where R&B doffed its roots to reach a wider and whiter audience.

Other 1954 highlights included the blues standard "I'm Your Hootchie Koochie Man"" (Muddy Waters) written by Willie Dixon, the doo-wop classics "Goodnight Sweetheart Goodnight" (The Spaniels) and "A Thousand Stars" (The Rivileers), the latter group featuring future acting sensation Lou Gossett Jr., "Mr. Sandman" (The Chordettes), "Tweedlee Dee" (Lavern Baker) and "Ling

Ting Tong" (The Five Keys).

SHAKEOUT #2

THE YOUTH CULTURE ARRIVES

1955-1963

During 1955 white American teenagers suddenly confronted images of their generation in two landmark movies – "The Blackboard Jungle" and "Rebel Without a Cause". The first film opened and closed with "Rock Around the Clock" (Bill Haley & The Comets) which weeks later became the first rock & roll record to reach #1 on the Billboard Pop Chart signaling the commercial dawn of the rock & roll era. A flood of rock & roll acts, many black, followed including Fats Domino, Bo Diddley, Chuck Berry, The Platters and Little Richard.

Rock & roll had worked its way onto daytime and prime time radio where white teenagers adopted it as their own. During the next two years, the music would make an indelible impact in movies and network TV. White artists including Elvis Presley, Buddy Holly, Rick Nelson and The Everly Brothers added to the white audience appeal.

The youth culture pervaded all areas of American life. Advertisers adopted a "think young" policy to reach both the young and people who wished they were. Dance crazes like the twist spread from high school sock hops to high society. Senator John Kennedy was elected President in 1960 with a vision of the future that excited American youth.

As the youth culture spun eagerly ahead, the losers in this shakeout were the roots artists like Wynonie Harris and early deejays like Alan Freed who had taken the risks to make rock & roll possible. They died forgotten or totally unknown by a new generation wholly unaware of their contribution.

1955

It had been a white adult world. In 1955, the arrival of the youth culture and the Civil Rights Movement caused more change to the social order than many could handle.

The movie "The Blackboard Jungle" depicted juvenile delinquency in an interracial high school. Even if the teenagers were troubled and confused, it was the first time that teenage characters had been the central focus of a movie. At that moment, a youth culture was born.

Months later, a second film, "Rebel Without a Cause" starring James Dean, framed the feelings of a teenager searching for the answer to what it takes to become a man. Dean perished in a violent car crash at age 24 just two weeks before the movie premiered giving the film an added poignancy.

"The Blackboard Jungle" left its own lasting impression with the anthem "Rock Around The Clock" which went directly to the Billboard Pop Chart where on July 9, 1955 it became the first rock & roll hit to reach #1 Pop. "Rock Around The Clock" made an even greater impact as the first rock & roll hit that drew everyone's attention, marking the commercial dawn of the rock & roll era.

At the same time that the youth culture was affirming itself, the Civil Rights Movement was addressing the brutal murder of teenager Emmitt Till and the indignity shown to seamstress Rosa Parks who refused to give up her seat to a white woman on an Alabama bus. Till's murderers cheated justice and even bragged about it years later in a Life Magazine interview, so the Rosa Parks dustup became a line drawn in the sand. The Montgomery bus boycott led by Dr. Martin Luther King, , Jr. was a moment of long deferred justice, not just for blacks but for people everywhere.

In this new social atmosphere, the Billboard Pop Chart opened wider than ever before to a variety of black artists including Fats Domino reaching Pop with his 25th single "Ain't That A Shame", Chuck Berry's road race hit "Maybellene", doo-wop going mainstream with The Platters on "Only You" and "The Great Pretender", straight blues from Little Willie John's "All Around The World", The Cadillacs as one of the first groups to employ well defined stage choreography with "Speedo" and Little Richard's outrageous scat talk on "Tutti Fruitti".

Of all the black artists, none landed with the immediate impact of Bo Diddley with his two sided hit "Bo Diddley" backed with "I'm A Man". The latter was the first raw blues by a black artist to make the Pop Chart, the former would become the most widely appropriated rhythm of rock & roll in subsequent hits such as "Not Fade Away" (Buddy Holly), "Willy And the Hand Jive" (The Johnny Otis Show), "Hey Little Girl" (Dee Clark), "I Want Candy" (The Strangeloves), "Magic Bus" (The Who),

"Faith" (George Michael), "Black Horse And The Cherry Tree" (K. T. Tunstall) and "Faster" (Matt Nathanson). Rock & roll's first major rhythm!

Even Billboard's Country Chart was undergoing a revolution as the outlaw country movement took hold with "Sixteen Tons" (Tennessee Ernie Ford) and "Folsom Prison Blues" (Johnny Cash) with their grittier social reality, while Elvis Presley's fourth Sun single "Baby Let's Play House" reach #10 Country and the follow-up "I Forgot To Remember To Forget #1 Country!

Other events fed into the youth culture. On March 28 at the Institute of Radio Engineers Convention in New York City, the transistor radio was first introduced making music portable while providing the earplug for late night listening.

On April 8, Alan Freed presented his "Rock & Roll Easter Jubilee" at Brooklyn's famed Paramount Theater featuring The Moonglows, The Penguins and Lavern Baker. Freed's Easter and Christmas concerts stoked the fire beyond what radio alone could do.

The Charts filled with a diverse range of pop and R&B acts including "See You Later Alligator" (Bill Haley & The Comets), "I Got A Woman" (Ray Charles), "Flip Flop & Fly" (Joe Turner), "Whole Lot-ta Shakin' Going On" (Big Maybelle Smith), "At My Front Door" (The El Dorados), and two more songs penned by Leiber & Stoller – "Smokey Joe's Café" (The Robins) and "Black Denim Trousers And Motorcycle Boots" (The Cheers). In Texas, the regional hit "Down The Line" by Buddy & Bob featured 17-year-old Buddy Holly in one of his first recordings.

The adult world, still firmly in control of the Pop Chart, reacted with disgust and bewilderment at these changes in the social order. Crooner Mel Torme couldn't understand why teenagers would prefer three chord rock & roll to the more intricate arrangements of jazz, while Frank Sinatra labeled rock & roll "the music of cretinous goons". Columbia Records A&R exec Mitch Miller appealed to the disc jockeys of America to find the courage to play other forms of music.

Living Blues Magazine reprinted this disclaimer which was widely circulated during the mid-50s – "Help save youth of America. Don't buy Negro records. The screaming idiotic words and savage music of these records are undermining the morals of our white youth in America. Call the advertisers of the radio stations that play this type of music and complain to them".

But there could be no turning back now. White teenagers ill served by the world of their parents were creating a culture of their own. During the next year, rock & roll would grow larger than any adult could have possibly imagined.

1956

White parents, religious groups, intellectuals and racial segregationists were united in their shared hope that rock & roll would blow over as a quick fad. Those hopes came crashing down in 1956 with the arrival of Elvis Presley. When Elvis made the jump from the Sun label to

RCA Victor, his new employer surrounded him with the best musicians and songwriters, sparing no expense to make this succeed.

The plan was deceptively simple. Five hit singles – "Heartbreak Hotel" backed with "I Was The One" (the top hit on the Billboard Pop Chart for 1956), "I Want You I Need You I Love You" backed with "My Baby Left Me", "Hound Dog" backed with "Don't Be Cruel" (the only hit to top the Pop, Soul and Country Charts simultaneously), "Blue Suede Shoes" and "Love Me Tender". Two LPs – "Elvis Presley" and "Elvis". A movie "Love Me Tender". And a total of 11 national TV appearances on "Tommy and Jimmy Dorsey's Stageshow", "The Milton Berle Show", "The Steve Allen Show" and "The Ed Sullivan Show".

At this junction, white teenagers fell in love with everything Elvis—the guitar, sideburns, sneering lip, two octave echo chamber voice, hips in orbit. His youthful energy, manners, religious leaning and light skin took him where black performers couldn't go—into white American homes. Only Elvis could pull off the balancing act of social rebel and loving son, a new Cadillac owner still indulging in the pleasures of youth—a mashed banana and peanut butter sandwich, at times an unknown commodity, at other times just one of us. Elvis mixed the elements of surprise and familiarity. Once Elvis was established, so was rock & roll. His star power kept it afloat long enough for others to complete the picture.

As Elvis reached the Pop Chart with RCA, his previous label Sun Records also broke through on the Pop Chart with "Blue Suede Shoes" backed with "Honey Don't" (Carl Perkins) and "Ooby Dooby" (Roy Orbison).

Capitol Records staged a national contest to discover the next Elvis. The winning entry "Be Bop A Lula" (Gene Vincent & The Blue Caps) communicated as much with heavy breathing as with words. Even Elvis' old school chum, Johnny Burnette, cashed in with his landmark single "Train Kept A Rollin'" backed with "Honey Hush", the first use of fuzztone guitar (an effect the singer stumbled upon when a tube worked loose in an amp).

Besides Elvis, 1956 would be remembered as the year that Hollywood went rock & roll with movies like "Shake Rattle And Roll" starring Joe Turner and Fats Domino and the Jayne Mansfield film "The Girl Can't Help It", the first color rock & roll film, featuring Fats Domino singing "Blue Monday", Gene Vincent performing "Be Bop A Lula", Little Richard's wild rendition of "Ready Teddy" and Eddie Cochran making his national debut with "Twenty Flight Rock".

Disc jockey Alan Freed portrayed himself in three separate movies that year—"Rock Around The Clock" starring Bill Haley & The Comets and The Platters, its sequel "Don't Knock The Rock" starring Haley and Little Richard and the star studded "Rock Rock Rock" with Chuck Berry, Johnny Burnette, The Flamingoes, Lavern Baker and Frankie Lymon & The Teenagers.

Freed also made radio history on April 7 when the CBS Radio Network first broadcast his series "The Rock And Roll Dance Party", network radio's first program devoted to rock & roll. "Cut-away" novelty records debuted with "Flying Saucer" (Buchanan & Goodman) where comedians would pose a question that would always be answered by a snippet from a popular song.

It was a year for saxophone blowouts including "Harlem Nocturne" (Earl Bostic), "Honky Tonk Part 1" (Bill Doggett) and "Rib Joint" (Sam Price), James Brown's first national hit " Please Please Please," the blues standard "Smokestack Lightning" (Howlin' Wolf), the English skiffle craze with "Rock Island Line" (Lonnie Donnegan), the classic last dance ballad "Goodnight My Love" (Jesse Belvin), "Fever" (Little Willie John), "Long Tall Sally (Little Richard) and "Roll Over Beethoven" (Chuck Berry) which spent only a single week in the top forty in spite of its now legendary status.

In Nashville, the Decca label dropped Buddy Holly & The Three Tunes after two unsuccessful singles. Holly would rebound to international fame the following year on Coral, a subsidiary of Decca.

In Philadelphia, deejay Bob Horn was fired as the host of the local television dance program "Philadelphia Bandstand", the result of both a drunk driving conviction and payola. In his place, the series recruited another deejay from WFIL—a clean cut 26-year-old Dick Clark.

1957

Seemingly as provincial as Lawrence Welk or Mitch Miller, "The Adventures of Ozzie & Harriet" on ABC TV did the unthinkable on April 10, 1957, transforming a 16-year-old Rick Nelson into the first rock star born from a role on a regular weekly TV series. Among his hits that year were "Be Bop Baby", "If You Can't Rock Me" and "Stood Up" backed with "Waitin In School". It lent an air of legitimacy to rock & roll for Ozzie & Harriet to risk their standing with older viewers to launch Rick's singing career.

It also made ABC TV the network that took risks that the competition wouldn't. On May 4, the network presented "The Alan Freed Show", a summer replacement series that made history as the first weekly television program devoted entirely to rock & roll. The debut show featured performances by Screamin' Jay Hawkins, The Del-Vikings and The Clovers.

Sensing the opportune moment, Dick Clark and the ABC TV affiliate in Philadelphia convinced the network to carry their afternoon teen dance program under the rechristened name "American Bandstand". It debuted August 5 featuring The Chordettes as the first musical guests. With many of the trappings of the local series such as guests lip-syncing their hits and the teenage studio audience rating the new record releases, "Bandstand" became the first rock & roll series with a long-term commitment from a TV network.

Even without TV, rock & roll was moving beyond R&B to attract a larger white audience with songs that addressed the teenage culture. "That'll Be The Day" (Buddy Holly), his breakthrough hit, was just that type of song. Holly based his work on a strong anticipation of the future and a belief that if people are honest and work toward their goal, success will come their way. To Holly, the worst obstacles were only temporary setback, never defeat. His 1957 hit "Everyday" was a breathless run toward the future while savoring every minute along the way.

If Holly provided the philosophy, The Everly

Brothers provided the voice, a harmony style so fluid that it was impossible to distinguish Phil from Don. Cadence Records paired the Everlys with the husband and wife songwriting duo Felice and Boudeleaux Bryant who created snapshots of the teenage state like "Wake Up Little Susie" concerning the pending wrath of overly judgmental parents. The Byrds, Simon & Garfunkel, and the Bo Deens were just a few of the later rock acts that patterned vocal performances after the style of the Everlys.

While Nashville had the Everlys, Memphis resonated with the pumping piano style of Jerry Lee Lewis. With his outlaw demeanor and suggestive lyrics, Lewis was capable of almost anything on stage including one incident where he doused the piano with a flammable liquid and set it ablaze just to outdo the following act. His version of "Whole Lotta Shaking Going On" topped at #3 Pop while the follow-up "Great Balls of Fire" reached #2 Pop, the two biggest hits for the Sun label.

In spite of the new talent, Elvis Presley was still the central figure in rock & roll. His hit "I'm All Shook Up" took the honor as the #1 hit on the Billboard Pop Chart for 1957, while a series of songs written by Leiber & Stoller added to his legacy – "Loving You," "Jailhouse Rock" backed with "Treat Me Nice" and "Don't". The movie "Jailhouse Rock" was Elvis' best rebel role as an ex-convict who scales the show business ladder by stepping on everyone he knows.

1957 was the year of the Frederick Kohner novel "Gidget" about a teenage girl in love with a surfer. The year that Little Richard abruptly retired from show business after a plane in which he was riding caught fire over the

Philippines. The year of the movie "Mr. Rock & Roll" starring Alan Freed, Chuck Berry, Little Richard, Clyde McPhatter and The Moonglows.

Also on the Chart that year was the Leiber & Stoller hit "Searchin" (The Coasters), "Rockin' Pneumonia And The Boogie Woogie Flu" (Huey Piano Smith), "Love Letters In The Sand" (Pat Boone), "Susie Q". (Dale Hawkins), "School Days" (Chuck Berry), "Come Go With Me" (The Del-Vikings), "Black Slacks" (The Sparkletones) and Sam Cooke's first national hit "You Send Me".

In Los Angeles, legendary disc jockey Hunter Hancock was the first to air "Louie Louie", the "b" side of a regional hit by Richard Berry. By playing the song on the hour, every hour at KGFJ, Hancock made it a bona fide west coast hit and a pillar of rock in subsequent incarnations.

On December 28, Alan Freed's Paramount Theater Christmas Concert revolutionized the presentation of rock. It was the first time anywhere that Screamin' Jay Hawkins rose from a coffin onstage to sing his sinister voodoo hit "I Put A Spell On You". His performance that evening in full vampire regalia pushed the stage presentation light years beyond the usual bump and grind to a new level of rock & roll theater.

1958

At the height of his career on March 24, 1958, Elvis Presley was inducted into the Army and sent to Germany. His movie "King Creole" was released shortly afterward, but Elvis would remain mostly out of the public view for the remainder of his military service while RCA did the best it could to parcel out the few unreleased Elvis songs it had.

Other acts did their best to fill the void. Chuck Berry had one of his most creative years with "Sweet Little Sixteen" backed with "Reelin' and Rockin'", Johnny B. Goode backed with "Round and round" and "Carol", songs delivered in tight staccato rhythm utilizing every syllable while defining rock & roll guitar. These were the riffs that would be copied by every kid who picked up a guitar for the next twenty years.

Buddy Holly brought his hyperventilating vocal "the Holly hiccup" and his brush-and-broom guitar style (striking the note while gently stroking the chord) to an impressive array of hits including "Maybe Baby" backed with "Tell Me How", "Midnight Shift", "Rave On", "Think It Over", "It's So Easy" and "Heartbeat" backed with "Well All Right". His pioneering use of the Fender Stratocaster guitar literally put the company on the map and the guitar in the hands of rock legends for the next thirty years.

Several songs defined 1958. "Summertime Blues" (Eddie Cochran) established the teenage agenda—a car, a no-hassle job and someone to love. The decade's most famous saxophone hit "Tequila" (The Champs) paved the way for other Chicano acts like 17-year-old Ritchie Valens who followed later that year with "Come On Let's Go" and "Donna" backed with "La Bamba".

Big problems were mounting. During a concert tour of England, Jerry Lee Lewis' career was left in limbo after the media learned of his marriage to his 13-year-old second cousin Myra. Bookings, record sales and TV appearances ground to a halt as conservative quarters branded him the scourge of American youth. A German concert tour by Bill Haley & The Comets ended in riot every time the group played "Rock Around The Clock".

A New York City powerhouse, Atlantic Records, stood perilously close to bankruptcy after a year without a solid hit. Just when they were needed the most, two singles on the Atlantic subsidiary Atco reached the Top Ten on the Chart – "Yakety Yak" (The Coasters) and "Splish Splash" (Bobby Darin) – putting the company back in the black.

Alan Freed made a quick rebound from a May 3 concert in Boston that turned into a rout. The police stopped the show and demanded that the lights be left on after the audience continued to dance in the aisles even after several warnings. It was widely reported that Freed took the mic and told the audience "Hey, kids, the police don't want you to have a good time". Several stabbings and muggings were reported following the concert, and Freed was indicted for starting a riot.

When WINS refused to support Freed publicly, he quit, resurfacing one week later on rival station WABC. His clout still intact, Freed gave a career boost to aspiring singer John Ramistella rechristening him Johnny Rivers and helping him to get his first contract with Gone Records where he enjoyed the modest hit "Baby Come Back".

Another indication of the weariness gripping music surfaced when Los Angeles radio station KCLA dispatched disc jockey Art Laboe to Scrivener's Drive In Restaurant for a live remote. Instead of asking for the latest hits, the customers requested songs from the past which Laboe dubbed "oldies but goodies". It had been less than four years since rock's commercial breakthrough and already a segment of people were clamoring for the better times that had slipped away. Laboe founded Original Sound Records, the first label devoted to reissued rock hits, and the "Oldies But Goodies" album series.

1958 would be remembered as -- the year that Little Richard entered divinity school at the same time that his hit "Good Golly Miss Molly" streaked up the Chart; Disc jockey Dick Biondi arrived at WLS Chicago challenging the tight playlist and other management constraints; "Volare" (Domenico Modugno) sung entirely in Italian became the top hit on the Billboard Pop Chart for the year; Berry Gordy , Jr. penned "Lonely Teardrops" (Jackie Wilson); "Witch Doctor" (David Seville) introduced the accelerated voice effect destined to become The Chipmunks; a single that just missed the top forty "Hey Schoolgirl" (Tom & Jerry) launched the career of the duo that would later be known as Simon & Garfunkel.

"American Bandstand" transformed Dick Clark into television's rock & roll kingmaker. Connie Francis' single "Who's Sorry Now" soared after "Bandstand" exposure. Twangy guitar star Duane Eddy ("Rebel Rouser") also achieved his first success when Clark became his manager and purchased an interest in his label Jamie Records.

Danny & The Juniors followed Clark's advice to change the name of their song "Do The Bop" to the more commercially viable "At The Hop," and Jerry Lee Lewis' moribund single "Breathless" catapulted to #7 Pop after

Clark's on-air promotion for viewers to send 50 cents along with five Beechnut Gum wrappers for a copy of the single.

To compete against "Bandstand", WNET TV, New York City, launched its own afternoon teen dance program "The Big Beat" hosted by Alan Freed mimicking on a local level what "Bandstand" was doing nationally. The program created a public outcry when Frankie Lymon, lead singer of The Teenagers, was shown dancing with a white girl. But the problem ran deeper than that. For Freed to revert to the role of a follower should have been the first hint of trouble on the horizon.

1959

A little after 1:00 a.m. on February 3, 1959, a light plane slammed into a snow covered farm field six miles north of Clear Lake, Iowa killing Buddy Holly, 22, Ritchie Valens, 17 and J. P. Richardson "The Big Bopper", 28. They had just completed a concert at the Surf Ballroom in Clear Lake and were en route to their next engagement.

For the next thirty years the world would attempt to come to grips with the enormity of the loss – from the "Peggy Sue" intro to Tommy Roe's "Sheila" (1962) to The Bobby Fuller Four's cogent imitation of the Holly guitar style on "I Fought The Law" (1966); the movies "The Buddy Holly Story" (1978) and "La Bamba" (1986); the scene in "American Hot Wax" (1978) where a sympathetic Alan Freed (Tim McIntyre) consoles the president of the Buddy Holly fan club on the anniversary of the crash; the character in "American Graffiti" (1973) who laments that there hasn't been any good music on the radio since Buddy

Holly died; Don McLean's "American Pie" (1971) which called it "The Day The Music Died".

Posthumous Holly tracks continued to surface through 1966 including the singles "True Love Ways" (1960), "Brown Eyed Handsome Man" (1963) and "Love's Made A Fool of You" (1964), each reminding us what could have been. The Crickets, now a group without a leader, backed The Everly Brothers on "Til I Kissed You" (1959) while Valen's label Del-Fi groomed Chan Romero as the next Chicano star with his high energy rocker "The Hippy Hippy Shake" (1959), a cult song that enjoyed legendary status in subsequent performances by The Beatles and The Swingin' Blue Jeans.

To many it seemed as if the heart had been torn out of the music, leaving it to the throes of the teen idol, perfunctory white kids with perfect hair and straight teeth whose looks alone could elicit the screams of teenage girls. "16 Magazine" debuted a mid year to cover the spectacle while "American Bandstand" brought it into American living rooms with a vanguard of Philadelphia singers that included Frankie Avalon, Fabian and Bobby Rydell. Clark owned an interest in several record companies including the Swan label which existed primarily to make a star of Philadelphia native Freddy Cannon ("Tallahassee Lassie"). Also at this time, disc jockey "Cousin" Brucie Morrow of WABC Radio began his concerts at Palisades Park, New Jersey featuring the top acts on the Pop Chart, inspiring the 1962 Freddy Cannon hit "Palisades Park".

It wasn't just the tragedy in Iowa. Other forces were tearing at the music. Alan Freed began the year with a role in the movie "Go Johnny Go" featuring performances by

Chuck Berry, Eddie Cochran, Ritchie Valens and Jackie Wilson. On November 20, Freed was fired by WNET TV and his program "The Big Beat" became history after his refusal to sign a waiver denying any involvement with payola. The following day, WABC Radio gave Freed the boot. The Miami Herald newspaper broke the payola scandal nationally with its headline "Booze, Broads, Bribes" following a notorious disc jockey convention in that city. Congress was about to take notice.

Troubles were multiplying for Chuck Berry. When a white woman hugged and kissed him during a concert in Meridian, Mississippi he fled town under the glare of national publicity. During December, Berry was booked for violation of the Mann Act regarding a teenager he had transported from Texas to work in his St. Louis club, a charge that would result in a 20-month prison sentence ending in 1963.

The social turmoil affected a drift in music. "The Battle of New Orleans" (Johnny Horton), a pure country song, was the top hit on the Billboard Pop Chart for 1959. At this point, jazz made a serious attempt to take back the hip young audience in hits like "What's I Say?" (Ray Charles), "Mack The Knife" (Bobby Darin) and two versions of "The Peter Gunn Theme" by Henry Mancini and Ray Anthony. Jazz soundtracks were embraced by a variety of TV shows aimed at young audiences including "77 Sunset Strip" and "The Many Loves of Dobie Gillis", and few characters on TV were more hip than Edd "Kookie" Burns and Maynard G. Krebs.

But rock & roll wasn't giving up. Leiber & Stoller had one of their most successful years penning "Love

Potion #9" (The Clovers), "Kansas City" (Wilbert Harrison) and a string of hits for The Coasters including "Charlie Brown", "Along Came Jones", "Poison Ivy" and "I'm A Hog For You". Songwriters Doc Pomus & Mort Shuman emerged with "Husabye" (The Mystics) and "There Goes My Baby" (The Drifters) while Berry Gordy , Jr. penned another hit, "You Got What It Takes" (Marv Hubbard).

Two enduring rhythms debuted – "Memphis" (Chuck Berry) and "(Baby) Hully Gully" (The Olympics), songs that would replicate in countless hits. Sun Records did its last major business with "Mona Lisa" (Carl Mann) and "Lonely Weekend" (Charlie Rich) while rock pioneer Hank Ballard released "The Twist", a dance craze initially ignored which would break open the following year.

Rock's first full decade drew to a close with the bobby soxer hit "Lipstick On Your Collar" (Connie Francis), the religious revival fervor of "Shout!" (The Isley Brothers), the last dance instrumental "Sleepwalk" (Santo & Johnny), the surrealistic blues/doo-wop hit "I Only Have Eyes For You" (The Flamingos), and the beatnik coffee house anthem "Bongo Rock" (Preston Epps).

1960

During August, 1960, a Philadelphia singer, Chubby Checker, utilized the launch pad of "American Bandstand" to send his cover version of "The Twist" to #1 on the Billboard Pop Chart. Soon the dance was everywhere from high school sock hops to high society. Teenagers first popularized the step, but it was the adults who kept it rolling for several years, viewing The Twist as a franc... for youth at any age.

R&B legend Hank Ballard, who had written and recorded the song a year earlier, had to resign himself to the fact that the public would always view the song as a Chubby Checker hit, this in spite of Ballard's breakthrough on the Pop Chart in 1960 with "Finger Poppin' Time" and "Let's Go Let's Go Let's Go".

Besides The Twist, the other big choreographed event was the discharge of Elvis Presley from the Army on March 5. Elvis shocked RCA executives by declaring his intention to sing opera. A compromise was worked out when the Italian opera piece "O Solo Mia" was transformed into the Elvis hit "It's Now Or Never", but mostly he stayed with ballads like "Are You Lonesome Tonight?" emphasizing maturity and a cleaner image that muted much of his spontaneous sexuality. Presley's career blueprint for much of the 60s was to avoid TV and to release two to three movies a year, gleaning most of his hits from soundtracks.

It wasn't just Elvis. Music was taking a decidedly softer tone. The Top Hit on the Billboard Pop Chart for 1960 "Theme From 'A Summer Place'" (Percy Faith) was a strange junction between a teen romance movie and the neo-classical music of the adult world.

One of the most successful groups to emerge from the turn toward pop was The Drifters featuring all new personnel. Ben E. King guided the group through a series of Doc Pomus-Mort Shuman ballads that included "This Magic Moment", "Save The Last Dance For Me" and "I

Count The Tears". Other 50s stars found greater commercial success with ballads and light novelty hits including Roy Orbison ("Only The Lonely") and Johnny Burnette (You're Sixteen").

Institutionalizing rock put out much of the fire as much as the caution from the payola scandal which broke wide open during 1960. Congressional hearings traced the flow of money from record companies buying their way onto airwaves, a common practice during the 1950s. Dick Clark survived with his reputation intact, but Alan Freed pled guilty and was eventually driven from radio. Disc jockey Arnie "Woo Woo" Ginsburg paid his fine and returned to WMEX, Boston where he held court for years afterward as if nothing had happened.

In the aftermath, new dynasties were building. Berry Gordy , Jr. began the year by adding to his songwriting credits with the hit "Money" (Barrett Strong). With $700 that he had borrowed from relatives, Gordy established Motown Records, destined to be the most successful label of the decade. At year's end, Motown achieved its first national hit "Shop Around" (The Miracles).

At this same time, The Shirelles were leading the charge of the 60s girl groups with "Will You Love Me Tomorrow" written by the husband and wife songwriting team of Carole King and Gerry Goffin. Employed at The Brill Building, 1650 Broadway in New York City by Aldon Music, a firm run by Don Kirshner, King & Goffin and two other successful songwriting duos, Jeff Barry & Ellie Greenwich and Barry Mann & Cynthia Weil, wrote hundreds of top forty hits during the 1960s and 70s; creating tailor made songs to the specifications of the artists who walked into this modern day tin pan alley shopping for success, a frantic and comical process later documented in the Broadway musical "Leader Of The Pack" and the 1996 movie "Grace Of My Heart".

1960 was the year The Everly Brothers departed the Cadence label for a 10-year contract with Warner Brothers and hits like "Cathy's Clown". Garage bands learned to play guitar by imitating the clean lines of The Ventures on "Walk Don't Run". Ray Charles formed a bridge between country and soul with "Georgia On My Mind". Bo Diddley had his second massive riff, "Road Runner". The blues classic "Fannie Mae" (Buster Brown). Jerry Butler and Curtis Mayfield teamed to write Butler's hit "He Will Break Your Heart". And novelty hits like "Ally Oop" (The Hollywood Argyles) and "Itsy Bitsy Teenie Weenie Yellow Polka Dot Bikini" (Brian Hyland) which utilized a cowbell to simulate a girl's sexy walk.

1961

At the peak of The Drifters' popularity, lead singer Ben E. King departed for a solo career with hits like "Spanish Harlem", co-written by Phil Spector and Jerry Leiber, and the formidable Leiber & Stoller ballad "Stand By Me". King's immediate impact would still be eclipsed by The Drifters' longevity.

1961 would be remembered as Rick Nelson's signature single "Hello Mary Lou" backed with "Travelin' Man". "Hello Mary Lou" briefly recaptured a hint of the 50s rockabilly while "Travelin' Man" served as a precursor to music videos. Unlike the usual "Ozzie & Harriet" show performance with Rick and the band in suits, "Travelin' Man" showed Rick singing the song while a changing panorama of locales and women's faces flashed across the TV screen. Originally, "Travelin' Man" had been trash-canned by Sam Cooke's manager, only to be rescued from oblivion by Rick's bass player, Joe Osborn, who brought it to Rick's attention.

1961 was the second consecutive year that The Twist held steady. Chubby Checker sang "Let's Twist Again" and starred in the movie "Twist Around The Clock". Joey Dee & The Starlighters offered their variation "The Peppermint Twist". At year's end, Chubby Checker's 1960 hit "The Twist" made an unexpected return to the Chart. Meanwhile, Checker's label Parkway launched a second big dance craze, "The Bristol Stomp" (the Dovells), featuring the lead vocal of 19-year-old Len Barry.

It was a year of strong hits, but few enduring trends. "Tossin' And Turnin'" (Bobby Lewis) was the #1 hit on the Billboard Pop Chart for 1961. Well defined rock songs like this and "Quarter To Three" (Gary U.S. Bonds) and "Little Sister" (Elvis Presley), written by Pomus & Shuman, were more the exception to the rule as the musical drift continued from 1960.

Among the best remembered hits of 1962 were "Crying" (Roy Orbison), the Motown hit "Please Mr. Postman" (The Marvelettes), "Mama Said" and "Baby It's You" by The Shirelles (the latter penned by Burt Bacharach and Hal David), "Last Night" (The Mar Keys) – the house band on so many Memphis soul recordings later in the decade, "Mother In Law" (Ernie K. Doe) and "I Like It Like That" (Chris Kenner) both penned by Allen

Touissaint, the dean of New Orleans songwriters, and "Where The Boys Are" (Connie Francis), an anthem to spring break at Fort Lauderdale.

Ray Charles continued spanning the universe from soul ("Hit The Road Jack") to lounge jazz ("One Mint Julep"). Some of the year's new names included The Pips featuring Gladys Knight ("Every Beat Of My Heart"), The Impressions with Curtis Mayfield ("Gypsy Woman") and the skinny kid with the vocal timber, Gene Pitney ("Town Without Pity").

Even as John Kennedy assumed the Presidency and filled the youth of America with his vision of the Peace Corps and the space program, an undercurrent of 50s nostalgia kept pulling the country back musically. "Peanut Butter" (The Marathons) was nothing more than a reworking of "(Baby) Hully Gully". "Honky Tonk Part 2" (Bill Doggett), a bigger sax blowout than the 1956 original. "Daddy's Home" (Shep & The Limelights), a continuation of The Heartbeats' 1956 hit "A Thousand Miles Away," both groups featuring the lead vocal of James Sheppard. "I Hear You Knockin'" (Fats Domino), a three-year-old track that finally found success as a single. And Little Caesar & The Romans wrapping up that longing for the old days with their hit "Those Oldies But Goodies".

Just as President Kennedy was moving the nation ahead socially, the musical doldrums of the early 60s would find their spark in a foreign group that no one in America had heard of in 1961. A wild guitar version of the children's song "My Bonnie Lies Over The Ocean" by the English group Tony Sheridan & The Beat Brothers became a hit in Germany, but nowhere else during the summer of

1961. Like the rest of the world, America had no way of knowing that this moment represented the beginning of a major trend that would soon sweep music worldwide, the first commercial breakthrough for a band that was already making its name on the English club scene. The Beatles.

1962

They didn't call James Brown the hardest working man in show business for nothing. His feet appeared to swivel in all directions in a fluid movement across the stage, rolling and turning in ways that the human body isn't supposed to. He was limber enough to outdo anyone at backbends or the splits, but his swiveling feet were his trademark.

Add to this his flair for stage theatrics. James would unexpectedly drop to his knees singing "Please Please Please", convincing the audience that he had collapsed from exhaustion. As he strained to keep the performance going with what little he seemed to have left, a rescuer would appear onstage, drape a cape around his shoulders and help a haggard James to hobble away. When the two were nearly offstage, Brown would throw off the cape and return to center stage with more strength than ever to conclude the performance.

During 1962, James Brown decided not only to perform his physically challenging act for the world's most demanding audience at New York's Apollo Theater, but also to invest $5,700 of his own money to capture that performance on record. "James Brown Live At The Apollo" spent 66 weeks on the R&B Chart, the first major live album in rock history. Many soul stations simply let the album track through. College fraternity houses added to the buzz. All this just two years prior to Brown performing the same act on "Shindig" and in the movie "The T.A.M.I. Show". Listening to the album you couldn't see his wild gyrations and theatrics, but the performance of Soul Brother #1 and the reaction of the audience made the live album a major force in rock & roll for years to come.

"The California Sound" took root as "Surfin'" (The Beach Boys) on the tinyCandix label went national during January. Not only was it the first song about the sport, it was the pop culture's introduction to the west coast lifestyle, a considerable influence for the remainder of the decade. Capitol signed The Beach Boys by mid-year, resulting in the follow-up hit "Surfin' Safari".

Transplanted New Yorker Phil Spector had already launched his Phillies label in Los Angeles based on his "wall of sound" recording technique, where components of a song are overdubbed until drumbeats resemble thunder and individual instruments were indiscernible. The 1962 hit, "He's A Rebel" (The Crystals), was an early example of this style.

Some trends held steady. "The Twist" (Chubby Checker) had returned to the Pop Chart during November, 1961, reaching #1 for a second time on January 13, 1962 making it the only hit in Billboard history to reach #1 on two successive runs. Twist fever continued unabated with "Twist And Shout" (The Isley Brothers), "Twistin' The Night Away" (Sam Cooke) and Chubby's second Twist movie "Don't Knock The Twist". But signs of overkill started to set in with albums like "Bo Diddley's A Twister,"

"Twistin' With Ray" (Ray Charles) and the single "Oliver Twist" backed with "Celebrity Twist" (Rod McKuen). Everyone was trying to cash in.

ABC TV made the decision to trim "American Bandstand" from an hour to thirty minutes prompting a threat from Dick Clark to quit the show. A massive letter writing campaign spurred in part by "16 Magazine" kept the show intact and Clark in charge.

The #1 hit on the Billboard Pop Chart for 1962, "Stranger On The Shore" (Mr. Acker Bilk), was a jazz instrumental from an English artist. "Telstar" (The Tornados), which paid tribute to the communications satellite that had just beamed the first television pictures across the Atlantic, was another English act reminiscent of The Ventures.

America was only seeing the tip of the English iceberg. In England, The Beatles started 1962 with a rejection from British Decca who instead hired the soft vocal harmony group The Tremeloes ("Silence Is Golden"). Later signing with EMI/Parlophone, The Beatles spent six weeks on the U.K. Chart with their first hit in England, "Love Me Do" backed with "P.S. I Love You". Since America paid little attention to trends in foreign countries, The Beatles were still unknown in the states.

Instead, America embraced the social relevance in folk music like "Where Have All The Flowers Gone?" (The Kingston Trio); added a harmonica player to every rock band after "Hey Baby" (Bruce Channel); considered the lonely road life of a rock star in "Teenage Idol" (Rick

Nelson); took a last taste of doo-wop with "Duke Of Earl" (Gene Chandler); realized the need for urban escapism with "Up On The Roof" (The Drifters) written by King & Goffin; and savored a sound of the future with "Green Onions" (Booker T. & The MGs).

"Sweet Georgia Brown" (The Carroll Brothers), a funky spin on the 1920s standard, was soon employed by the media as a soundtrack to flashy basketball footage creating a new niche in rock & roll—the sports anthem. A half dozen more would follow during the century.

1963

On August 28, 1963, Dr. Martin Luther King , Jr. delivered his "I Have A Dream" speech to a massive gathering at the Washington, D.C. mall, a moment of triumph for The Civil Rights Movement. Less than three months later on November 22, President John Kennedy was assassinated in Dallas leaving the nation, particularly young people, to search for a new source of idealism.

Between these two defining moments, the musical buzz was "Louie Louie" (The Kingsmen), a remake of Richard Berry's 1957 song by the decade's foremost garage band. Garage bands took credit for originating obscure music or sampling forgotten songs in the music they did compose. At least a half dozen Kingsmen singles were guilty of this, making them the most successful example of the genre.

Because the lyrics to "Louie Louie" were unidentifiable or indecipherable, a rumor spread on college campuses that the words were obscene, leading to a year-and-a-half investigation by the FBI resulting in no firm conclusion. Besides that controversy, "Louie Louie" became many things in the years that followed including the frat rock anthem in the movie "Animal House" (1978) and the first song to spawn its own book, "Louie Louie" by Dave Marsh (1992).

The 3/2 rhythm of "Louie Louie" returned repeatedly in subsequent hits including "I'm A Fool" by Dino, Desi & Billy and "Just Like Me" by Paul Revere & The Raiders (both 1965), "Wild Thing" by the Troggs (1966), "Beg Borrow & Steal" by The Ohio Express (1967) and "Start The Commotion" by The Wise Guys (2001). The Sandpipers' MOR version of "Louis Louis" played off the melody, totally muting the rhythm.

Two trends dominated the Charts in 1963. Surf music reached its crescendo with "Surfin' U.S.A". (The Beach Boys), "Surf City" (Jan & Dean), "Wipe Out" (The Surfaris) and "Pipeline" (The Chantays). Franking Avalon and Annette Funicello released the first of five surf movies that summer, "Beach Party". Companion to this trend were the car hits including "Little Duece Coupe" (The Beach Boys) and "Hey Little Cobra" (The Rip Chords).

The other trend was the crest of the girl group sound with "My Boyfriend's Back" (The Angels), "It's My Party" (Lesley Gore), "He's So Fine" (The Chiffons), "Da Doo Ron Ron" (The Crystals), "Be My Baby" (The Ronettes), "Popsicles and Icicles" (The Murmaids), "Heat Wave" (Martha & The Vandellas) and "When The Lovelight Starts Shining Through His Eyes" (The Supremes).

Motown pulled The Supremes from the poverty of the Detroit housing projects, pairing them with the songwriting trio of Brian Holland, Lamont Dozier and Eddie Holland, resulting in twelve #1 hits for the group as the last girl group standing a decade's end.

These were the days that Top 40 AM Radio reached its zenith with powerhouse stations cranking up the amps at sundown to cover a wide swath of The United States. The result was regional hits. "Long Tall Texan" (Murray Kellum) reached #1 that summer on KOMA, Oklahoma City while not even making the playlist at another station in the Storz chain, WHB, Kansas City. At WLS, Chicago, it was "Elephant Walk" (Donald & The Delighters), a love story set in the impoverished Chicago south side. "These Arms Of Mine" (Otis Redding) introduced the soul legend throughout the south, while the west coast was buzzing with "Little Latin Lupe Lu" (The Righteous Brothers).

During December, 1963, Wolfman Jack (Bob Smith) began broadcasting on XERF 1570 AM located nine miles south of Del Rio, Texas in the small Mexican desert town of Via Cuncio. With a power output of 1 million watts at a time when American stations were limited to 50,000 watts, XERF blanketed North America bouncing its signal across the ocean to Europe and Russia. It was pirate radio, where anything could happen including an early episode where the previous station owners attempted to regain control with a gun battle that was fully audible on mic to a disbelieving audience.

Even the Beatles owed their American breakthrough to regional airplay. When the crude, unsynchronized footage of the group singing at The Cavern Club aired on

"The CBS Morning News" (November 22) and "The CBS Evening News With Walter Cronkite" (December 10), disc jockey Carroll James of WWDC, Washington, DC had Beatle records flown over from England, opening the first pocket of Beatlemania in America. That stunt, combined with the persistence of Beatle manager Brian Epstein and Capitol Records A&R exec Dave Dexter, , Jr., resulted in the release of "I Want To Hold Your Hand" backed with "I Saw Her Standing There" on December 26, 1963. Garnering sales of 2,967,422 records in just five days, it signaled the hysteria about to engulf the nation.

And none too soon. The assassination of President Kennedy cast a pall over the holiday season, evidenced in the tearful ballad "In The Summer Of His Years" (Connie Francis). 1963 would be remembered for the emergence of songwriter Bob Dylan on the Peter, Paul & Mary hits "Blowin' In The Wind" and "Don't Think Twice It's All Right'" ; for the first all female rock band Goldie & The Gingerbreads on the Decca label; for the experimental instrumentals "Memphis" (Lonnie Mack), "Jack The Ripper" (Lind Wray & The Ray Men) and "Out Of Limits" (The Marketts); for the #1 hit on the Billboard Pop Chart for 1963 "Sugar Shack" (Jimmy Gilmar & The Fireballs) and other memorable moments including "On Broadway" (The Drifters), "Can I Get A Witness" (Marvin Gaye), "Another Saturday Night" (Sam Cooke), "It's All Right" (The Impressions) and "Um Um Um Um Um Um" (Major Lance) written by The Impression's Curtis Mayfield. Barely missing the chart "Harlem Shuffle" (Bob & Earl) would rebound as a hit in England during 1969.

SHAKEOUT # 3

ENGLAND, WOODSTOCK AND STUDIO 54

1964-1980

A nation looking for renewal after the assassination of President Kennedy found it in The Beatles and the other English Invasion groups that flooded America with their infectious optimism in 1964. This sudden re-ordering of musical priorities dislodged many acts from the Pop Chart including Chubby Checker, The Everly Brothers and Rick Nelson, while Elvis Presley endured three full years without a gold single.

At this same time, R&B of the 50s was transformed into the more sophisticated soul sound by everyone from James Brown to Motown. Each year brought a new musical style – surf music, folk rock, Tex-Mex, bubblegum, psychedelic, jazz-rock. The music matured into social statements against war and racism. Album rock was born with "Highway 61 Revisited" (Bob Dylan) and "Rubber Soul" (The Beatles) in 1965, bringing its impetus to FM radio while AM Top Forty during the 70s had its last surge of popularity with disco.

Three centers of social activity now lost to time remain vibrant in the imaginations of music lovers from this era – the early to mid-60s England that launched The Beatles and other groups; the weekend that was "Woodstock", the most famous concert in rock history; the late 70s excess of Studio 54 in New York City where social limits were left in the dust.

A number of icons died during this era from drugs and other excesses, but the crashing blow occurred on December 8, 1980 when John Lennon was assassinated outside his apartment in New York City. The Beatles had brought us back to reality after JFK's death. Seventeen years later we had come full circle, thanks to another murder. Who would get us through this?

1964

Two weeks after the Chart appearance of "I Want To Hold Your Hand" (the top single on the Billboard Pop Chart for 1964), the public discovered a second Beatles single, "She Loves You", that had been quietly sitting in record stores since September, 1963. This broke the one-hit jinx suffered by most foreign acts in America, that and the fact that The Beatles sang in English which American teens could understand.

What followed was a flood of singles by The Beatles which defied all laws of oversaturation. Among the records they set: the most Top Forty hits in a year (19), the most #1 hits in a year (6), and during the week of April 4, The Beatles held down the top five positions on the Billboard Pop Chart, a feat no other performer has equaled.

For the first time in history, England was viewed as a trendsetter in music and fashion. The Beatles haircut combed forward in a dry, natural style quickly replaced the greased pompadour. The group's matching outfits and jodhpur boots were copies by every fey imitator. As singer/songwriters they opened the recording studio to every form of experimentation. Their energetic guitar work and vocals in difficult keys set them apart from the American norm.

Besides revitalizing music, The Beatles helped us to move on with life only weeks after the Kennedy assassination, while opening the door to The English Invasion which during 1964 alone included Dusty Springfield, The Dave Clark Five, The Searchers, Gerry & The Pacemakers, Peter & Gordon, The Overlanders, Billy J. Kramer & The Dakotas, The Swingin' Blue Jeans, Chad & Jeremy, The Animals, The Kinks, The Rolling Stones, Manfred Mann, The Honeycombs, Herman' Hermits, The Zombies and The Hollies.

The effect of all this was equally jarring to both countries. Previously successful American acts like Chubby Checker, The Orlons and Rick Nelson couldn't find their place in the shakeout. Some retired while others retreated to Nashville to modernize C&W. In England, a pirate station Radio Caroline began broadcasting from a ship just beyond territorial waters at 12:00 noon on Sunday, March 29 signing on with "Can't Buy Me Love" (The Beatles) and offering a slate of rock acts that the BBC wouldn't touch – Georgie Fame, The Rolling Stones, The Animals, The Yardbirds. As Caroline and a half dozen other shipboard stations sprung up, their combined influence resulted in the BBC liberalizing its programming.

Back in America, the cliché was 'if it wasn't English it was Motown', as the label had its most successful year yet with The Supremes ("Baby Love"), The Temptations ("The Way You Do The Things You Do"), The Four Tops

("Baby I Need Your Lovin'"), Mary Wells ("My Guy"), Martha & The Vandellas ("Dancing In The Street"), Marvin Gaye ("How Sweet It Is") and The Marvelettes ("Too Many Fish In The Sea").

Both English and American acts joined forces October 28/29, 1964 at The Santa Monica Civic Auditorium to film the first rock concert movie "The T.A.M.I. Show (Teen Age Music International)" featuring The Beach Boys, The Supremes, The Rolling Stones, Chuck Berry, Gerry & The Pacemakers, Lesley Gore, Jan & Dean, Billy J. Kramer & The Dakotas, Marvin Gaye, The Barbarians, and Smokey Robinson & The Miracles. None of the other acts wanted to follow James Brown who was led from the stage three times only to come bounding back for another chorus of "Please Please Please". After a single TV performance in 1972, "The T.A.M.I. Show" remained hidden away until its March, 2010 DVD release. The Library of Congress entered it in its National Film Registry during 2006.

ABC TV premiered its cerebral prime-time concert series "Shindig!" on September 16, 1964 making instant stars of its regulars The Righteous Brothers, Glen Campbell, Bobby Sherman and the girl dancer with the oversized glasses – Carol Shellene. NBC TV would respond four months later with its own concert series "Hullabaloo".

1964 will be remembered as the year that soul great Sam Cooke, 29, was shot to death in an L.A. hotel; "My Boy Lollipop" (Millie Small) gave America its first taste of Caribbean ska; the discotheque craze took off with the album "Johnny Rivers Live At The Whiskey A Go Go";

Terry Stafford confounded the experts with his uncanny Elvis impersonation on the doc Pomus-Mort Shuman tune "Suspicion" which had previously been recorded by Elvis; Jerry Leiber & Mike Stoller's Red Bird Records hit with the girl groups The Shangri Las ("Leader Of The Pack"), The Dixie Cups ("Chapel Of Love") and The Jelly Beans ("I Wanna Love Him So Bad") – hits penned at The Brill Building.

It was the year of the blues standard "Hi Heel Sneakers" (Tommy Tucker) ; Memphis Soul on the Hi label from Gene Simmons ("Haunted House") and Willie Mitchell ("20-75"); the gospel hit "Amen" (The Impressions); the summer smash "Under The Boardwalk" (The Drifters) and "Oh, Pretty Woman" (Roy Orbison), featuring his two trademarks – the tiger growl and the exclamation, "Mercy!".

Dick Clark moved "American Bandstand" from Philadelphia to L.A., closing off Philly's most important national media outlet. Almost immediately, local record labels began folding. The previously formidable Cameo/Parkway continued through the summer of 1967 with declining results.

1965

It was the year America fought back to regain control of the Pop Chart from the English onslaught with several music derivatives including Tex-Mex (elements of Spanish and Anglo music) on hits like "Wooly Bully" (Sam The Sham & The Pharoahs) – the #1 hit on the Billboard Pop Chart for 1965, "She's About A Mover" (The Sir

Douglas Quintet) and "Treat Her Right" (Roy Head).

Folk-rock became another dominant style with "Laugh Laugh" (The Beau Brummels), "The Sounds of Silence" (Simon & Garfunkel), "Mr. Tambourine Man" (The Byrds) and "It Ain't Me Babe" (The Turtles), the latter two written by Bob Dylan. Impressed by the rock versions of his songs, Dylan crossed over to rock as well with the album "Highway 61 Revisited", its six minute single "Like A Rolling Stone" and tracks like the 12-minute allegory of Nazi German "Desolation Row" which blew the lid off constraints for length, content and presentation.

Although years behind the folk music movement, rock & roll was exploring protest music and social commentary on a variety of hits including "(I Can't Get No) Satisfaction" (The Rolling Stones), "Universal Soldier" (Donavan), "A Well Respected Man" (The Kinks) and the apocalyptic "Eve Of Destruction" (Barry McGuire) written by P.F. Sloan.

America's escalating involvement in Vietnam was the main lightning rod for protest. Two of folksinger Pete Seeger's peace anthems, "Where Have All The Flowers Gone" and "Turn Turn Turn", became big hits for Johnny Rivers and The Byrds, respectively.

Not to be outdone by the changes taking place, The Beatles released the LP "Rubber Soul", the first rock album to reach #1 without a Top Forty hit, although several of its tracks became as legendary as their hits – "In My Life", "Michelle" and "Norwegian Wood". Anticipating this trend, WOR FM, New York City, inaugurated its progressive format during April, 1965, a format with no jingles, no deejay patter over song intros, lengthy sets of music and announcers speaking in a normal conversational tone. The birth of album rock.

Flying in the face of this trend, Bill Drake launched the "boss radio" format at KHJ, Los Angeles, pairing the playlist down from 50 records to 35 and giving tighter rotation to the bigger hits. The lines were now drawn for the war between AM and FM, which would continue through the 70s.

A second wave of English performers reached the American Chart in 1965, including The Who ("Kids Are Alright"), Georgie Fame ("Yeh Yeh"), The Moody Blues ("Go Now"), the first snarl of acid rock guitar with The Yardbirds ("Heart Full Of Soul") and The Fortunes ("You've Got Your Troubles") penned by Roger Cook and Roger Greenaway whose songwriting would exert considerable impact well into the 70s.

Milestones for the year included "My Girl" (The Temptations) written by Smokey Robinson and recorded on stage at The Apollo Theater; James Brown at his peak with "Papa's Got A Brand New Bag" and "I Got You (I Feel Good)"; "We Gotta Get Out Of This Place" (The Animals), one of the most legendary moments in songwriting at The Brill Building capturing The Animals' rise to fame from the hardscrabble mining town of Newcastle; "I Got You Babe" (Sonny & Cher) and "Shaking All Over" (The Guess Who), the first U.S. hit for Canada's top rock group.

On November 6 in San Francisco, Bill Graham opened The Fillmore Auditorium with a concert featuring

The Grateful Dead, Jefferson Airplane and The Charlatans.

Elvis Presley would have his last gold record for three years with "Crying In The Chapel". Like other roots acts, Elvis would feel the turnaround in fortunes brought on by The Beatles. Around 10:00 p.m. on August 27, 1965, The Beatles dropped by to meet Elvis at Presley's Bel-Air Mansion. The five staged a three-hour jam session with the tape recorder rolling, a legendary performance that has yet to surface.

For 25 cents and two box tops from Kellogg's Corn Flakes, music fans could obtain a true 60s oddity—the 45rpm single of "Doin' The Flake" (Gary Lewis & The Playboys), a song that never charted and never made it to the radio. Gary, the son of comedian Jerry Lewis, was enjoying a string of Chart hits that included the 1965 summer smash "Save Your Heart For Me".

1966

Trouble was lurking everywhere. John Lennon's over-the-top remark that The Beatles were as popular as Jesus set off a spate of public record burnings and radio station bans, contributing to the group's decision to stop touring. Bob Dylan retreated from touring and recording for two years amid questionable reports of a motorcycle accident.

Twenty-five-year-old Jan Berry suffered severe brain damage in an automobile accident bringing a premature end to Jan & Dean. And The Bobby Fuller Four ("I Fought The Law") no sooner appeared than its namesake died from asphyxiation under suspicious circumstances.

College campus anti-war protests were mounting daily, yet the #1 hit on the Billboard Pop Chart for 1966, "The Ballad Of The Green Berets" (Ssgt. Barry Sadler) took the adult pro-war position. This would be the last year that such a song would be possible.

Many acts absorbed the tension and tumult of the era and blasted their amps as a metaphor to the chaos and confusion – "19th Nervous Breakdown" (The Rolling Stones), "Eight Miles High" (The Byrds), "My Generation" (The Who), "Inside Looking Out" (The Animals), "The Great Airplane Strike" (Paul Revere & The Raiders) and "Happenings 10 Years Time Ago" (The Yardbirds) featuring both Jeff Beck and Jimmy Page in their only hit together.

The year wasn't all high decibel. With "Pet Sounds", The Beach Boys moved on to more mature statements like "Wouldn't It Be Nice" and "Caroline No". The group sought to undermine The Beatles dominance with their statement of spirituality "Good Vibrations", the first Top Forty hit to feature an electronic synthesizer.

Blue-eyed soul flared with The Young Rascals ("Good Lovin'") and 17-year-old Steve Winwood fronting The Spencer Davis Group ("Gimme Some Lovin'"); pouty Nancy Sinatra's I'm-so-sexy-so-what? Attitude sparked hit records "These Boots Are Made For Walkin'" and cult movies like "The Wild Angels", while your grandmother's 78s from the 1920s seemed in vogue again with "Winchester Cathedral" (The New Vaudeville Band).

On Monday, September 12, NBC TV debuted "The

Monkees", a small screen version of The Beatles. Their first three singles and first two albums shot to #1 due in part to Don Kirshner selecting the material for the band to record. In spite of a highly successful two-year run, the band took whatever job it could find after the series folded. By 1969 they were cloying as panelists on the daytime game show "The Hollywood Squares".

1966 was the most successful year for that New York jug band institution, The Lovin' Spoonful, with five major hits – "Daydream", "Did You Ever Have To Make Up Your Mind?", "Summer In The City", "Rain On The Roof" and "Nashville Cats", while lead singer John Sebastian's composition "Younger Girl" became a top hit for The Critters. The Hollies also came into their own with "I Can't Let Go", the summer romance hit "Bus Stop" and belly dancer classic "Stop! Stop! Stop!".

Among the lyrics that framed the year, "California Dreamin'" (The Mamas & The Papas) drew a generation to the west coast; "Mother's Little Helper" (The Rolling Stones) cast a stark depiction of middle class drug addiction; "The Dangling Conversation" (Simon & Garfunkel) chronicled a disintegrating relationship while "Cherish" (The Association) spoke of a relationship that never progressed beyond the longing phase.

Among the year's hot trends – ABC TV's hip satire "Batman" sent the "Batman Theme" up the Chart in versions by Nelson Riddle, Neal Hefti and The Marketts; the debut of cassette tapes, spelling doom to its troubled cousin the 8-track; the movie debut of the decade's hottest sex symbol, Raquel Welch, in the rock & roll film "A Swingin' Summer" featuring The Righteous Brothers, Gary

Lewis & The Playboys and The Rip Chords.

1966 will be remembered for Neil Diamond's debut with "Solitary Man"; for the impossibly simple arrangement of "96 Tears" (? & The Mysterians); for "Gloria" (Them featuring Van Morrison); and "Secret Agent Man" (Johnny Rivers) written by P. F. Sloan for the TV series of the same name.

When Coral Records released the album "Holly In The Hills" featuring the last unreleased tracks of Buddy Holly, rumors abounded that he was still alive and just hiding out. Most of the tracks were from his earliest recordings as a teenager, not as polished as his later work.

1967

1967 dawned with acts like Peter & Gordon, Nancy Sinatra and Mitch Ryder & The Detroit Wheels topping the Chart, but by year's end, all had been swept aside by the social force alluded to in the hits "San Francisco (Be Sure To Wear Flowers In Your Hair)" (Scott McKenzie) and "San Franciscan Nights" (The Animals).

The summer of love had arrived at the corner of Haight and Ashbury Streets with hippies, tye-died fashions, love beads, communal living, peace insignias, KMPX FM and the debut of Rolling Stone Magazine.

For many it came together June 16-18 at The Monterey International Pop Festival headlined by The Byrds, The Animals, Simon & Garfunkel and The Mamas & The Papas. Here the baton was passed to the icons of the hippy era—Janis Joplin and Jimi Hendrix—while in the audience was 33-year-old Columbia Records A&R exec Clive Davis who blew the lid off the stodgy record giant by signing Joplin and The Grateful Dead.

Hendrix pioneered feedback guitar, pulling impossible sounds from his amp while using his thumb as a fifth finger to play the background and lead simultaneously. Joplin's instrument was her voice, conveying power and anguish while bringing the hard lessons of life to each performance.

Those unable to travel to California found the flower power music as close as their radio with "White Rabbit" (Jefferson Airplane), "Light My Fire" (The Doors), "Foxey Lady" (Jimi Hendrix), "I Can See For Miles" (The Who) and "Incense And Peppermint" (The Strawberry Alarm Clock). Even pop stalwarts incorporated elements of the experimental and avant-garde in hits such as "It's Wonderful" (The Rascals), "Susan" (The Buckinghams) and "Wild Honey" (The Beach Boys).

In this open climate albums were increasing the gap between AM and FM, "Sgt. Pepper's Lonely Hearts Club Band" (The Beatles) stretched the perimeters of music with adventurous tracks like "A Day In The Life", "Being For The Benefit Of Mr. Kite" and "Lucy In The Sky With Diamonds", The Moody Blues took serious music further with "Days Of Future Past", the first album to blend classical music and rock together without doing a disservice to either. The Rolling Stones created one of the year's standout tracks, "2,000 Light Years From Home", using the moog synthesizer to simulate outer space drift.

Even the professional stage felt the first ripple of the movement on October 29 at The Public Theater in East Greenwich Village in New York City when the world witnessed the first performance of the hippy musical "Hair" with its litany of songs destined for Top Forty success – "Hair," "Easy To Be Hard," "Good Morning Starshine" and "Aquarius/Let The Sunshine In".

In spite of the positive atmosphere, tragedy intruded on December 10 when a plane carrying soul legend Otis Redding, 26, went down in an icy lake near Madison, Wisconsin, drowning Redding and four band members. It had only been six months since his triumph at Monterey Pop and less than a month before the release of "(Sittin' On) The Dock Of The Bay," his only #1 Pop Hit.

Otis wrote "Respect" which Aretha Franklin took to the top of the Charts in 1967. Although not originally written as an anthem to women's empowerment, it was transformed to that level by Aretha demanding her due while not diminishing her man in the process. Aretha's four octave range filled the airwaves that year with the hits "Baby I Love You," "Chain of Fools" and the Carole King/Gerry Goffin masterpiece "(You Make Me Feel Like) A Natural Woman," establishing Aretha as one of the most important voices of her generation.

1967 would also be remembered for the blue-eyed soul classics "Groovin'" (The Rascals), "Then You Can Tell Me Goodbye" (The Casinos) and the Kenny Gamble/Lester Huff production "Expressway To Your Heart" (The Soul Survivors); "The Beat Goes On" (Sonny & Cher); the early music video "Strawberry Fields Forever" (The Beatles); "Sock It To Me Baby" (Mitch Ryder & The

Detroit Wheels); the top hit on the Billboard Pop Chart for 1967 "To Sir With Love" (Lulu); "Never My Love" (The Association); "Brown Eyed Girl" (Van Morrison) and from the influential L.A. club The Ash Grove, the emergence of The Nitty Gritty Dirt Band ("Buy For Me The Rain").

1968

In a world ablaze with hatred and violence, 1968 witnessed the assassinations of Dr. Martin Luther King, Jr. and Senator Robert Kennedy; violent race riots in Washington, D.C., Detroit and Los Angeles; dark events in Vietnam such as the Tet Offensive and My Lai; daily confrontations between antiwar protestors and the police, spilling over to The Democratic National Convention in Chicago where protestors violently repelled by the police chanted, "The whole world is watching!".

With social cacophony so widespread, psychedelic music became the soundtrack of the times; "In-A-Gadda-Da-Vida" (Iron Butterfly); "Piece Of My Heart" (Big Brother & The Holding Company); "Pictures of Matchstick Men" (Status Quo); "All Along The Watchtower" (Jimi Hendrix); "The Shape Of Things To Come" (Max Frost & The Troopers); "Magic Bus" (The Who).

The acid wave witnessed the emergence of Ten Nugent in The Amboy Dukes ("Journey To The Center Of The Mind"); the return of former Yardbirds' guitarist Eric Clapton fronting the trio Cream ("Sunshine Of Your Love"); the melody of The Kinks' "All Day And All Of The Night" returning with The Doors ("Hello I Love You"); and the motorcycle anthem "Born To Be Wild"

(Steppenwolf) which gave loud rock of the 70s its name in the lyric "I Like smoke and lightning, heavy metal thunder...".

Against this backdrop of social upheaval, the #1 hit on the Billboard Pop Chart for 1968, "Hey Jude" (The Beatles), was a song of reassurance. Its flip side, "Revolution", stressed the need for social responsibility. Taken together, the two songs represented an attempt to sort the truth from the rhetoric, providing people pause to think through their feelings.

AM radio's answer to the social storm clouds, bubblegum music, targeted pre-teens with its depiction of kissing games and girls as sweet as gum drops. Neil Bogart of Buddah Records developed The 1910 Fruitgum Company ("1-2-3 Red Light"), The Ohio Express ("Yummy Yummy Yummy") and The Lemon Pipers whose hit "Rice Is Nice" was the first mass-released stereo single. CBS TV brought the bubblegum sound to Saturday mornings with the cartoon "The Archie Show" produced by Don Kirshner, resulting in hits like "Bang Shang A Lang".

Yet confrontation seemed the rule of the day. At KSAN Radio, San Francisco, the parent company Metromedia fired the entire deejay staff over the profanity in the songs "The Pusher" (Steppenwolf) and "Eskimo Blue Day" (Jefferson Airplane). The staff resurfaced later at a competing station.

Although he seemed out of place in these times, Elvis Presley re-emerged with his first million selling hit in three years, "If I Can Dream", followed on December 3 by his one-hour NBC TV concert special "Elvis!" (later known as the comeback special). This was his first TV appearance in over eight years.

At the movies, "The Graduate" presented a May/September romance with a Simon & Garfunkel soundtrack that included "Mrs. Robinson" and "Scarborough Fair". The Fillmore East opened in New York City on March 8. America received its first taste of reggae with "Hold Me Tight" (Johnny Nash) and one of the last moments of the old Motown glamour when The Temptations and The Supremes teamed to sing "I'm Gonna Make You Love Me".

New acts included Creedance Clearwater Revival ("Susie Q".), The Bob Seger System ("Ramblin' Gamblin' Man"), Three Dog Night ("Nobody") and from the L.A. club The Ash Grove, the hippy blues band Canned Heat ("Going Up The Country").

The Philadelphia sound ruled soul music, whether it was Thom Bell producing The Delfonics ("La La Means I Love You") or Kenny Gamble/Lester Huff productions of The Intruders ("Cowboys To Girls") and Jerry Butler ("Only The Strong Survive). In Nashville, former Roy Orbison producer Fred Foster worked the same comeback magic with Ray Stevens who finally received his due as a serious songwriter with "Unwind" and "Mr. Businessman".

Among the other highlights of 1968 – "Jumpin' Jack Flash" (The Rolling Stones); "The Weight" (The Band); "Stormy" (The Classics IV); "Everyday People" (Sly & The Family Stone); "Who's Making Love" (Johnnie Taylor); "The Beatles" (universally known as the white album) and the Byrds' LP "Sweetheart Of The Rodeo," the cradle of country rock.

1969

450,000 converged on White Lake, New York on August 15 for the Woodstock Festival serving notice that a better way had to be found other than the status quo of war, racism and environmental neglect. At 3:24 p.m. that Friday afternoon, folksinger Ritchie Havens led off the concert with a two-hour improvisational set.

The concert concluded the following Monday morning with Jimi Hendrix's performance, which included his controversial rendition of "The Star Spangled Banner" complete with the simulated sound of airplanes dropping bombs, a moment that served as a flashpoint in the generation gap for years to come. Although Hendrix didn't mention Vietnam, he didn't have to, jacking up the amps for peace so that it could be heard all the way to the White House.

Folksinger Joan Baez took the more plaintive track with her ballad about union organizer "Joe Hill" while Country Joe & The Fish openly baited the war machine with the inflammatory "Feel Like I'm Fixin' To Die Rag".

The concert featured emerging acts including Santana, Joe Cocker, Mountain, Melanie, Crosby Stills & Nash, Sha Na Na, Ten Years After, Arlo Guthrie and Sweetwater, as well as established acts such as Janis Joplin, Jefferson Airplane, The Who, The Grateful Dead, The Band, Sly & The Family Stone, Canned Heat, Creedance

Clearwater Revival and Blood, Sweat & Tears.

Governor Nelson Rockefeller threatened to deploy The National Guard to close down the concert until organizers talked him out of it. More than 400 were treated for drugs. There were two deaths and one birth. A severe downpour which the audience not only survived but made a sport of afterward in the mud. Nudity. Social abandon. Yoga. A new food called granola. The 1970 film "Woodstock" by Michael Wadleigh, as well as two albums of performances, preserved the legacy. "Woodstock" was the moment we learned there were more of us than them.

Creedance Clearwater Revival, a group that made no references to sex or drugs, dominated the Chart in 1969 with tales of paddle-wheelers ("Proud Mary"), rural southern life ("Green River," "Born On The Bayou"), bands playing just for the fun of it ("Down On The Corner") and a unique hit contrasting world apocalypse to a hoedown tempo ("Bad Noon Rising").

The legendary concept album "Tommy" (The Who) told the story of a deaf, dumb and blind boy who discovered fulfillment at the controls of a pinball machine. It featured the hits "Pinball Wizard", "I'm Free" and "See Me Feel Me" and enjoyed a rebirth as a 1975 movie.

In deference to previous musical trends sparked by small independent record companies, the giant Columbia label spearheaded the jazz-rock movement with Blood, Sweat & Tears ("Spinning Wheel"), The Spiral Starecase ("More Today Than Yesterday") and The Chicago Transit Authority ("Questions 67 & 68").

Diana Ross departed The Supremes with their

prophetic swan song "Someday We'll Be Together" while Peter, Paul & Mary called it quits with the John Denver song "Leavin' On A Jet Plane". The Beatles recorded their final album "Abby Road" (although "Let It Be" would be released afterward.

Comebacks included both Bob Dylan ("Lay Lady Lay") and Rick Nelson & The Stone Canyon Band ("She Belongs To Me") in a country rock vein; The Sir Douglas Quintet ("Mendocino") and The Zombies ("Time Of The Season"). The latter group had disbanded in 1968. Their hit was a 1967 track finally reaching single status.

Former members of The Byrds, The Hollies and Buffalo Springfield formed the new super group Crosby Stills & Nash ("Suite: Judy Blue Eyes"). The Guess Who signed with RCA and broke big with "These Eyes", "Laughing" and "Undun" while Led Zeppelin, the model metal screamers for the 70s, debuted with "Whole Lotta Love".

Two weeks after astronaut Neil Armstrong became the first man to set foot on the moon, folk legend John Stewart captured the moment with "Armstrong" while the album "In The Court Of The Crimson King" (King Crimson) was released, a landmark album essential to every underground radio station's library.

1969 would also be remembered for the bubblegum classic "Sugar Sugar" (The Archies), the #1 hot on the Billboard Pop Chart for 1969; "Hot Fun In The Summertime" (Sly & The Family Stone); "Honky Tonk Women" (The Rolling Stones); "Sweet Caroline" (Neil Diamond); "Traces" (The Classics IV) and "Think" (Aretha

Franklin).

Those familiar uncredited voices singing "It's the real thing" on the Coca Cola commercials were The Fortunes. The mid-60s group was about to make another run at the Pop Chart.

1970

If we all just pull together, it's all going to work out fine. That optimistic credo swept through the lyrics of dozens of hits during 1970, including some with a spiritual or ecological undertone.

Songs like "Bridge Over Troubled Water" (Simon & Garfunkel), the top hit on the Billboard Pop Chart for 1970; "He Ain't Heavy He's My Brother" (The Hollies); "Let It Be" (The Beatles); "Teach Your Children" (Crosby Stills Nash & Young); "Everything Is Beautiful" (Ray Stevens); "New World Comin'" (Mama Cass Elliott); "United We Stand" (The Brotherhood Of Man); "Share The Land" (The Guess Who); "Ooh Child" (The Five Stairsteps); "Easy To Be Free" (Rick Nelson & The Stone Canyon Band); "Let's Work Together" (Canned Heat); "Out In The Country" (Three Dog Night); "Spirit In The Sky" (Norman Greenbaum) and "Raindrops Keep Fallin' On My Head" (B. J. Thomas).

Those lofty platitudes didn't always gel with reality. The killing of four students during an antiwar rally at Kent State University on May 4 dealt a fatalistic blow to the peace movement, inspiring the Crosby Stills Nash & Young hit "Ohio". The deaths of Jimi Hendrix and Janis Joplin both at 27 from drug overdoses left the hippy culture on equally shaky ground. And "creative differences" caused both The Beatles and Simon & Garfunkel to call it quits, ending a major part of 60s mindset.

Anyone listening could hear the first strains of the 70s in the electrified samba of the Santana hits "Evil Ways" and "Black Magic Woman"; the bubblegum soul of The Jackson Five("I Want You Back"); the psychedelic sound of Sly & The Family Stone ("Thank You Falettinme Be Nice Elf Agin"); pensive folksinger James Taylor ("Fire And Rain"); Beatle stepchild Badfinger ("Come And Get It"); Motowns' first white act Rare Earth ("Get Ready"); studio wunderkind Todd Rungren as Runt ("We Gotta Get You A Woman"); English blues band Fleetwood Mac ("Oh Well"); the romantic pop group Bread ("Make It With You") and Elton John with a halting lyric about a man too shy to articulate his love ("Your Song"). Even shock rocker Alice Cooper came crashing into the national consciousness as the band tearing up pillows in the party scene of the movie "The Diary Of A Mad Housewife", a preview of things to come.

Top 40 AM radio anointed Led Zeppelin ("The Immigrant Song") as the avatar of heavy metal, but FM album rock stations threw their weight behind the album "Paranoid" (Black Sabbath) featuring the overpowering guitar of Tony Iommi and menacing vocals of Ozzy Osbourne. "Paranoid" laid out the doom and hopelessness agenda that would drive heavy metal for the next three decades with subjects like nuclear annihilation, drug death and war mongers. Its singles hit "Iron Man", the story of a murderous robot running amok, featured one of the most famous heavy metal guitar riffs of all time.

The feel-good album for Top 40, "Cosmo's Factory" (Creedance Clearwater Revival), played out like a greatest hits package with the singles "Travelin' Band" backed with "Who'll Stop The Rain", "Up Around The Bend" backed with "Run Through The Jungle" and "Lookin' Out My Back Door". Under fire by the counterculture for sacrificing art to commercialism, the Top Forty format received an unexpected boost during the July 4 weekend with the premiere of the syndicated radio series "American Top 40" hosted by Casey Kasem, based on the listings of the Billboard Pop Chart.

On September 25, "The Partridge Family" debuted on ABC TV, based loosely on the 1960s rock family The Cowsills. It introduced teen idol David Cassidy and numerous hits beginning with the debut single "I Think I Love You".

But the counterculture was ready to cede nothing including AM radio. During the autumn of 1970, KAAY, Little Rock blanketed much of the United States and Canada with "Beeker Street" each night at 11:00 p.m. Hosted by Clyde Clifford, the show brought underground music to regions of the country where it was otherwise unavailable. The eclectic playlist on any evening could include King Crimson, It's A Beautiful Day, Traffic, jazz innovator Don Ellis, Mason Proffit, plus everything from the volatile comedy cut "Legend Of The USS Titanic" (Jaime Brockett) to dramatic readings like "Where It' At" (Leonard Nimoy).

Rock revival was also in the air. The radio syndication company Drake-Chenault, headed by former boss radio creator Bill Drake, premiered the 50-hour rockumentary "The History Of Rock & Roll" at the same time that the Solid Gold radio format was bringing the oldies back to radio.

The year's Chart anomaly belonged to English studio singers Tony MacAuley and Tony Burrows who hit the Chart under three separate aliases in four months – Edison Lighthouse ("Love Grows Where My Rosemary Goes"), White Plains ("My Baby Loves Lovin'") and The Pipkins ("Gimme Dat Ding").

Other highlights included the jazz-rock hits "Vehicle" (The Ides Of March), "Lucretia MacEvil" (Blood, Sweat & Tears) and "Make Me Smile" (Chicago); the blurring of sexual lines with "Lola" (The Kinks); and the legend of a struggling dancer "Mr. BoJangles" (The Nitty Gritty Dirt Band).

1971

It said what millions of women were feeling in the 1970s, and with its unique and intimate piano style, the album "Tapestry" (Carole King) sold 16 million copies, a preview of the massive amount of records that would sell during the decade. Divorced from her longtime songwriting partner, Gerry Goffin, King achieved success as a solo songwriter with the album's hits "It's Too Late" backed with "I Feel The Earth Move" and "So Far Away". James Taylor recorded his own version of another "Tapestry" track, "You've Got A Friend", making it one of the philosophical amalgams of the decade.

A 360 degree turn from all of this was the rise of

shock rocker Alice Cooper ("Eighteen") decapitating baby dolls on stage and Bloodrock's grisly gorefest "D.O.A." with disturbing images of severed limbs and death. Real death was also a sure sell. "Riders Of The Storm" (The Doors) took an even eerier connotation with the death of lead singer Jim Morrison, 27, in Paris on July 3. The mood piece seemed to connect the listener with Morrison in the great beyond.

The Janis Joplin album "Pearl" also resonated like a voice from the grave. Its single, "Me And Bobby McGee" reached #1 Pop while its ironically titled instrumental track "Buried Alive In The Blues" left fans to wonder what might have been if Janis had lived long enough to record the vocal track.

That same realm of the unknown sparked a brief interest in cryptic lyrics that could be interpreted in a myriad of ways. Some listeners analyzed every word of "American Pie" (Don McLean) and "Stairway To Heaven" (Led Zeppelin). The latter was even cited for its demonic messages when spun backwards. Neither act provided any confirmation for any of the theories floated about their songs, drawing more commercial mileage from the ambiguity.

1971 marked the beginning of the solo career of Rod Steward ("Maggy May"); the arrival of folksinger Carly Simon ("Anticipation"); moog synthesizer geniuses Emerson, Lake & Palmer ("Lucky Man") and the soul group The Stylistics ("You Are Everything") produced by Thom Bell; two new jazz-rock acts Chase ("Get It On") and Lighthouse ("One Fine Morning") and a big year for the city of Chicago with the breakthrough of The Chi-Lites

("Have You Seen Her?"); the debut of the syndicated television dance program "Soul Train" hosted by Don Cornelius and the birth of the influential blues label Alligator Records.

Hoyt Axton ruled the songwriting roost that year with "Joy To The World" (the top hit on the Billboard Pop Chart that year) and "Snowblind Friend" (Steppenwolf). Brewer & Shipley tested the waters for drug lyrics for AM radio with "One Toke Over The Line" while Marvin Gaye took Motown to a higher level of social involvement with "Mercy Mercy Me" (The Ecology) and "What's Going On?".

The 60s mindset was quickly receding. "Signs" (The Five Man Electrical Band) was one of the few confrontational lyrics to make the Top Forty that year, while the movie "Billy Jack" did what it could with the themes of racism, child abuse and the environment. Clearly "them vs. us" wasn't playing as well in the 70s. The Who said as much in "Won't Get Fooled Again", but the hard evidence came down with the final concert at the Fillmore East on June 27 and the closing of the Fillmore West one week later.

As one saga ended, another began. On June 14, The Hard Rock Café opened in London's Park Lane and weeks later when Eric Clapton donated a guitar to hang on the wall, the restaurant began amassing a collection of rock memorabilia so extensive that other branches would open worldwide just to showcase it.

1971 would also be remembered for "If" (Bread); the controversial Rolling Stones' album cover "Sticky

Fingers" featuring the likeness of a pair of jeans with a working zipper; "All I Ever Need Is You" (Sonny & Cher); "Me And My Arrow" (Nilsson) from the animated ABC TV Movie Of The Week "The Point"; "Imagine" (John Lennon); "Oye Como Va" (Santana); and the return of The Fortunes with the Roger Cook/Roger Greenaway composition "Here Comes That Rainy Day Feeling Again".

The Grass Roots utilized a unique marketing strategy for the single "Sooner Or Later" by including the call letters of stations like WHB (Kansas City) and WLS (Chicago) in the song's intro, knowing the stations would proudly air their personalized versions.

Quietly, Berry Gordy, Jr. began moving Motown Records to its new headquarters in Hollywood to facilitate the making of movies including "Lady Sings The Blues", "Mahogany" and "The Wiz". For aspiring Detroit performers, the Cinderella story ended here.

1972

If the decade hadn't previously affirmed itself, it did so during 1972 with the debut of major acts including The Eagles ("Take It Easy"), The Doobie Brothers ("Listen To The Music"), America ("I Need You"), Steely Dan ("Do It Again"), Yes ("Roundabout") and Jim Croce ("You Don't Mess Around With Jim").

The epic story song came into its own with "Taxi" (Harry Chapin) and "American City Suite" (Cashman &

West) while "Rock & Roll Part 2" (Gary Glitter) was quickly adapted by professional football teams to celebrate touchdowns, remaining the rock & roll football anthem for the remainder of the century.

Everyone speculated over "You're So Vain" (Carly Simon). Was it written about Warren Beatty or Mick Jagger? "Rocky Mountain High" (John Denver) sent thousands scrambling for the good life in Colorado, causing Denver to ask them to stop coming because they were destroying the environment. And that famous Coca Cola commercial with the peaceful congregation gathered on the mountaintop became the hit "I'd Like To Teach The World To Sing" (The New Seekers). It was written by English tunesmiths Roger Cook and Roger Greenaway who also penned "Long Cool Woman In A Black Dress" (The Hollies).

Stevie Wonder began a five-year experiment on the album "Music Of My Mind", employing the synthesizer and clavinet to create more depth and texture to his music. Another synthesizer masterpiece "Trilogy" (Emerson Lake & Palmer) slipped into classical music pretensions for which other albums of this era would be known.

The buzz rumor was that 1972 would experience a major musical turnaround based on the eight-year cycle established by Elvis and The Beatles. Hopes were pinned to both "Bang A Gong (Get It On)" (T. Rex) and "Go All The Way" (The Raspberries), two powerful pieces of guitar driven pop. But when neither group came up with a substantial follow-up, the hope fizzled leaving people to realize that 1972 would not be a landmark year.

It was a year a new generation said 'move over, Guy Lombardo'. With "American Bandstand" in its 15th year, Dick Clark began a new holiday tradition on December 31, 1972 when NBC TV presented "Dick Clark's New Year's Rockin' Eve" featuring Three Dog Night, Al Green, Helen Reddy, Billy Preston and Blood, Sweat & Tears. NBC only televised the concert the first two years, but ABC TV picked it up in 1974 carrying it into the next century.

Another TV milestone was the short-lived "In Concert" series which debuted on ABC TV on November 24, 1972 with an all star show featuring Alice Cooper, The Allman Brothers Band and Blood, Sweat & Tears. Produced by Don Kirshner, the show was syndicated as "Don Kirshner's Rock Concert" after its brief network run.

1972 would be remembered as the year that many old ideas came to fruition. "Layla" (Derek & The Dominoes), a two-year-old track and "Nights In White Satin" (The Moody Blues), a five-year-old album cut, both became Top Forty hits. Chuck Berry reworked a four-year-old album track, "My Tambourine", for his #1 hit "My Ding A Ling" while Rick Nelson turned the failure of a 1971 concert at Madison Square Garden into his #1 hit "Garden Party".

A Willie Dixon song that had been part of The Rolling Stones' repertoire since the mid-60s "I Just Want To Make Love To You" suddenly caught fire for Foghat. And some well-known names returned. Songwriter Leon Russell, this time as a performer with "Tightrope", and Sonny Geraci, former leader of The Outsiders, fronting the group Climax ("Precious And Few").

Of all the duration stories, none could top The Spinners, a soul group that had enjoyed only marginal success on a variety of labels for more than a decade. With the Atlantic label, The Spinners finally achieved stardom with "I'll Be Around" and "Could It Be I'm Falling In Love", songs recorded under the watchful eye of Thom Bell who was still producing two other acts, The Delfonics and The Stylistics, for two other labels.

It was the year Creedance Clearwater Revival released their last hit "Someday Never Comes" and David Clayton-Thomas left Blood, Sweat & Tears; Paul Simon achieved solo success with "Mother And Child Reunion" and "Me & Julio Down By The Schoolyard"; Alice Cooper's "School's Out" LP came wrapped in a pair of paper panties which brought the group a million dollars worth of free publicity when the record failed to clear English customs; and Motown forged forward with the gritty social vision of songwriters Barrett Strong and Norman Whitfield on "Papa Was A Rolling Stone" (The Temptations).

The #1 hit on the Billboard Pop Chart for 1972 was "The First Time I Ever Saw Your Face" (Roberta Flack), but the year would be remembered for a rich variety of other hits including "Lean On Me" (Bill Withers), "Saturday In The Park" (Chicago), "Crocodile Rock" (Elton John), "Morning Has Broken" (Cat Stevens), "Separate Ways" (Elvis Presley) and the popular album cut "Sentimental Lady" (Fleetwood Mac).

1973

"Tie A Yellow Ribbon 'Round The Old Oak Tree" (Tony Orlando & Dawn), the top hit on the Billboard Pop Chart for 1973, was historic in several ways. It served as a barometer for AM radio's feel good philosophy. It tied with "Yesterday" (The Beatles) as the most widely recorded song of all time with more than 3,000 versions. But above all, it served as a metaphor of hope in times of crisis. Beginning in 1979 with the Iranian hostage crisis and continuing through every national crisis since, Americans have adorned their trees and homes with yellow ribbons as a public demonstration for a positive outcome in troubled times.

The year's other major statement "The Cover Of The Rolling Stone" (Dr. Hook & The Medicine Show) savaged the warped mindset of self-involved rock bands and the culture that created them, resulting in the group being featured on the March 23 issue of Rolling Stone and leaving it to history to decide which of the two entities got the best of the joke.

1973 had been a phenomenally successful year for Jim Croce. The barroom rocker "Bad Bad Leroy Brown" coined the phrase "meaner than a junkyard dog", while a year-old ballad "Time In A Bottle" caught commercial fire after being featured in an ABC TV movie of the week "She Lives!" about a young woman dying of cancer.

Croce's final album "I Got A Name" released just prior to his death at age 30 in a plane crash presented the two types of songs that Jim did best – simple love ballads with thoughtful lyrics and humorous rock songs about blue collar people facing life with the hope that conditions have to improve because they can't get any worse. In the album's epilogue "The Hard Way Every Time", Jim put his life in perspective, leaving his fans to conclude that his brief time on the planet was filled with meaningful experiences.

The loss of Croce was tempered with a close call for soul legend Stevie Wonder. On August 6, Stevie slipped into a coma after a freak accident in South Carolina where a giant log broke loose from a lumber truck, smashing the windshield of the car that Stevie was traveling in and splitting his skull. After several days in a coma, Stevie regained consciousness showing no signs of mental impairment. His output for the year included "You Are The Sunshine Of My Life" and "Living For The City".

1973 was the year of the country rock war between Los Angeles groups like The Eagles, seemingly detached from any rural connection, and the country/blues style emanating from Atlanta and Jacksonville championed by The Allman Brothers Band ("Ramblin Man"), The Eagles claimed the greater commercial success with pieces such as "Desperado" which presented the themes of indecision and non-commitment, leaving it to the listener to apply the lesson learned. But the Allman Brothers Band released a definite candidate for best country rock album of all time with "Brothers And Sisters."

Soul music witnessed the rise of Philadelphia International, the label of Kenny Gamble and Lester Huff, featuring hits like "Love Train" (The O'Jays) and "If You Don't Know Me By Now" (Harold Melvin & The Blue Notes). But the real surprise was Gladys Knight & The Pips signing with the Buddah label just as their last Motown single "Neither One Of Us Wants To Say Goodye" became a top hit. At Buddah the group put together a string of hits written by Jim Weatherley (who penned "Neither One Of Us") including "Midnight Train To Georgia", "The Best Thing That Ever Happened to Me" and "Where Peaceful Waters Flow".

At Columbia Records an era drew to a close when its President Clive Davis was fired for mismanagement of funds, a charge for which he was later cleared. Davis had discovered and signed to the label Janis Joplin, The Grateful Dead, Blood, Sweat & Tears, Santana, Billy Joel, Aerosmith and Bruce Springsteen.

Among the concerts that made history during 1973 was "Elvis Aloha From Hawaii Via Satellite" (January 14) beamed to 1 and 1/2 billion viewers in twenty countries and The Watkins Glen Festival (July 29) in upstate New York which set a new attendance record of 600,000 that turned out to witness performances by The Grateful Dead, The Allman Brothers Band, and The Band, another milestone for legendary concert promoter Bill Graham.

1973 also featured hits like "China Grove" (The Doobie Brothers), "Hello It's Me" (Todd Rundgren), "Cisco Kid" (War), "Frankenstein" and "Free Ride" (The Edger Winter Group), "Stuck In The Middle With You" (Steeler's Wheel) produced by Jerry Leiber and Mike Stoller, and the first "Homegrown" LP from KGB Radio, San Diego, providing first exposure to local artists singing about area locales, a trend that later swept the nation. In the continuing search for an upgrade to audio quality, Quadrophonic momentarily flared. The concept of dividing a song among four speakers proved too ambitious for a listener with only two ears. In a matter of months, Quad fizzled.

1974

AM radio found a way to distance itself even further from FM with the first reverberations of disco on the hits "For The Love Of Money" (The O'Jays), "TSOP (The Sound of Philadelphia)" (MSFB), "You're The First, The Last, My Everything" (Barry White), "Love's Theme" (The Love Unlimited Orchestra) and "Rock The Boat" (The Hues Corporation).

Disco would create some unlikely stars. Monty Rock III had been a familiar guest on "The Tonight Show" for years trying to assimilate with every musical trend that appeared. In 1974, he transformed himself into a disco singer with the #1 Pop Hit "Get Dancin'" (Disco Tex & His Sex-O-Lettes).

Innovation was shifting away from radio with its canned formats to the dance club scene where a deejay still had the license to improvise. In the dance clubs of The Bronx, deejays like Afrika Bambaataa, Kool Herc and Pete "D.J." Jones began using a rhythmic patter to keep the pace going between records. Rap.

Other forces were pulling music in a myriad of directions. "Boogie On Reggae Woman" (Stevie Wonder) and "The Bitch Is Back" (Elton John) tested the limits of AM censorship. Eric Clapton introduced America to the music of Jamaican reggae legend Bob Marley when he made a hit of Marley's song "I Shot The Sheriff". A number of albums were so huge that they straddled both AM and FM including "Band On The Run" (Paul McCartney), the rock symphony "El Dorado" (Electric Light Orchestra) and "Verities And Balderdash" (Harry

Chapin), an album that featured both his standard "Cat's In The Cradle" and the well-known track "What Made America Famous?", a story of people pulling together in a crisis. The latter song was eventually made into a full-blown Broadway show.

Guitar legend Jeff "Skunk" Baxter departed Steely Dan following the release of "Rikki Don't Lose That Number", resurfacing immediately with The Doobie Brothers on their hits "Another Park Another Sunday", "Eyes Of Silver" and "Black Water". Steely Dan would spend the next three years regrouping.

Canadian music had its own transition underway. The Guess Who enjoyed their last major hit "Clap For The Wolfman", a tribute to Wolfman Jack featuring voice-overs from the deejay. Even as The Guess Who were fading, a second Canadian group, Bachman-Turner Overdrive, fronted by The Guess Who's former lead guitar player Randy Bachman was affirming itself with the hits "Takin' Care Of Business" and "You Ain't Seen nothin' Yet".

At the Eurovision Song Festival, one of Europe's largest music competitions, the Swedish group Abba beat out 7,000 competitors with their entry "Waterloo", which became a worldwide hit by year's end. It was also the year that two deposed record executives started their own independent labels. Clive Davis, former President of Columbia Records, launched the Arista label with romantic ballad singer Barry Manilow ("Mandy") while Neil Bogart, the record exec responsible for the Buddah bubblegum wave of the 1960s, founded Casablanca Records with the first album by the heavy metal group Kiss.

The #1 hit on the Billboard Pop Chart for 1974, "The Way We Were" (Barbra Streisand), was the theme from a nostalgic love movie set in the turbulent 60s which showed that the baby boomers were moving on with their lives.

1974 would also be remembered for "Come And Get Your Love" (Redbone), a two-year-old song "Lady" (Styx) achieving hit status, the desperate lounge performer in "Piano Man" (Billy Joel), "Come Monday" (Jimmy Buffett), the country inflection of "Fairytale" (The Pointer Sisters), "Wishing You Were Here" (Chicago) with backup vocals by The Beach Boys, and the song that defined 70s cuteness, "Muskrat Love" (America).

1975

Was rock & roll losing its edge? The #1 hit on the Billboard Pop Chart for 1975, "Love Will Keep Us Together" (The Captain & Tenille), was a happy pop song written by 60s teen idol Neil Sedaka whose own career was enjoying a resurgence with the hit "Laugher In The Rain".

Millions of albums were selling like never before resulting in "Captain Fantastic And The Brown Dirt Cowboy" (Elton John) becoming the first album in Billboard history to debut at #1! The LP "Fleetwood Mac" served as that group's commercial breakthrough with the hits "Over My Head", "Say You Love Me" and the tale of a witch who takes a mortal lover, "Rhiannon".

But where was the edge in 1975? The best examples were probably Bruce Springsteen's commercial breakthrough with "Born To Run", Queen ("Killer Queen"), Kiss ("Rock & Roll All Night") or Supertramp ("Bloody Well Right"). These moments were becoming few and far between.

AM radio continued in the disco vein with "Love To Love You Baby" (Donna Summer), "Jive Talkin'" (The Bee Gees), "Fly Robin Fly" (Silver Convention), "Theme From S.W.A.T." (Rhythm Heritage) and "Shame Shame Shame" (Shirley & Company).

The hip young audience began to turn elsewhere for its social bite. Comedy became the new stage for counterculture with the debut of NBC TV's "Saturday Night Live" combining cutting edge comedy with rock music challenging the limits.

The rock underground retreated to the gender-bending "Rocky Horror Picture Show". A commercial flop initially, it grew into the greatest midnight cult movie of all time, inspiring the audience to dress like characters in the film and re-enact the scenes in sync with the film.

During 1975 "Austin City Limits" debuted on PBS, providing a national springboard for acts like Stevie Ray Vaughan while chronicling the music of the last quarter of the 20th century including the only performance by blues legend Lightning Hopkins in color and stereo.

What few highlights the year had included The Jefferson Airplane reincarnated in the more mature sound of The Jefferson Starship ("Miracles"), America bowing out with the hits "Sister Goldenhair" and "Daisy Jane", 10CC's Messianic-like chorus for "I'm Not In Love", Michael Murphy's tribute to the horse "Wildfire", Elton John's homage to tennis great Billy Jean King "Philadelphia Freedom", Janis Ian's painful remembrance of an awkward adolescence "At 17", Bob Seger going to "Katmandu", and the Australian group Pilot turning in an amazing imitation of Paul McCartney & Wings with "Magic".

1976

Having a little fun with his own identity, Paul McCartney's "Silly Love Songs" (Wings) became the top hit on the Billboard Pop Chart for 1976 making him the first individual to sing on three separate hits to achieve that honor, the first two being The Beatles' hits "I Want To Hold Your Hand" (1964 and "Hey Jude" (1968).

The most unique single of the year "Bohemian Rhapsody" (Queen) was the first to combine opera with rock & roll, a tribute to the vocal calisthenics of the group. The heavy metal group Kiss achieved their biggest hit with the tender ballad "Beth" about a musician attempting to balance his personal life with the demands of his career. For sheer drama nothing could top the single "(Don't Fear) The Reaper" (Blue Oyster Cult) where a vampire closes in on his victim.

It was the year of the concert album "Frampton Comes Alive" (Peter Frampton) which became the first pre-recorded cassette tape certified for sales of a million copies. It featured "talk-box" guitar hits such as "Show Me The Way", "Baby I Love Your Way" and "Do You Feel Like We Do".

1976 was the year Paul Simon spoke for aging baby

boomers still trying to hang in there with "Still Crazy After All These Years"; The Steve Miller Band did some of its best work with the hits "Rock N' Me" and "Fly Like An Eagle"; The Starland Vocal Band ("Afternoon Delight") became the only 'one hit wonder' to host its own summer replacement TV series.

It was also the year of two separate versions of "It Keeps You Runnin'" by Carly Simon and The Doobie Brothers, nearly interchangeable; the year Don Kirshner launched his record label with "Carry On Wayward Son" (Kansas); and former Lovin' Spoonful leader John Sebastian had a #1 Pop Hit with the theme from the ABC TV sitcom "Welcome Back (Kotter)". In fact, ABC TV introduced its fall lineup with a series of promos based around "Still The One" (Orleans).

Among the new acts to bow during 1976 – Heart ("Magic Man"), Al Stewart ("Year Of The Cat"), and Firefall ("You Are The Woman"). Going solo for the first time were the former leader of The Guess Who, Burton Cummings ("Stand Tall") and ex-Raspberrie Eric Carmen ("Never Gonna Fall In Love Again").

It was also the year the small independent label Private Stock topped the Charts with "Moonlight Feels Right" (Starbuck) and "Did You Boogie (With Your Baby)" (Flash Cadillac & The Continental Kids) featuring voiceovers by Wolfman Jack.

The Pop Chart continued to thump with the disco beat with The Bee Gees ("You Should Be Dancing"), Silver Convention ("Get Up And Boogie"), Brick ("Dazz"), Abba ("Dancing Queen") and The Spinners ("Rubberband

Man").

Other highlights from 1976 included the first #1 hit for Chicago, "If You Leave Me Now", the Bruce Springsteen song "Blinded By The Light" (Manfred Mann's Earth Band), and Bachman-Turner Overdrive doing tasty jazz licks with "Lookin' Out For #1".

Life Magazine's special Bicentennial issue "The 100 Events That Shaped America" included such milestones as the telephone, the Salk vaccine and The Declaration of Independence along with two moments from rock & roll—the arrival of The Beatles (1964) and Woodstock (1969).

1977

On the afternoon of August 16, 1977 when the news flashed worldwide that Elvis Presley, 42, had died, disbelief gave rise to panic as millions of fans descended upon every record store and Wal-Mart literally clearing his records from the shelves including many moribund titles that hadn't moved in years.

Finding it impossible to keep pace with the demand, RCA hired additional employees to keep the record pressing plants operating around the clock until the market eventually softened. At the time of his death, Elvis' 114 Chart hits had contributed to sales of 500 million records worldwide. In the three years following his death, and additional 500 million records were sold (as many as during his 23-year career) for a total of 1 billion records.

It was learned later that a decade of prescription drug abuse had shut down Presley's colon and intestines. He died in the bathroom at Graceland unable to discharge waste, a sad end for a remarkable life.

With the public mourning the loss of Presley, a second tragedy occurred on October 20 when a twin engine plane made a forced landing in a Mississippi swamp killing three members of Lynard Skynard including lead singer Ronnie Van Zant, 28. Although most of the band survived, it would never recapture its mid-70s prominence when hits like "Sweet Home Alabama" and "Free Bird" placed it in the pantheon of southern rock.

Seemingly a world away from these negative events, the trendy dance club Studio 54 opened on April 26 at 254 West 54th Street, New York City. The social vision of its owners Steve Rubell and Ian Schrager, the club combined all of the elements of disco which people grew to love or hate—throbbing lights, music, sex, drugs, fashion chic and celebrity. To attain this formula, Rubell and his employees enforced a strict entry policy, keeping the public waiting outside behind a velvet rope in the frequently futile hope of being selected for entry.

Celebrities including Andy Warhol, Liza Minelli and Mick Jagger were quickly ushered in. Fashion sense and attitude were also a ticket inside since fashion designer Halston and "People Magazine" were feeding off the spectacle. Soon the club developed a reputation worldwide for flaunting societal constraint, whether it was the notorious celebrity orgies in the well-guarded basement or the open sex and cocaine use taking place in full sight on the main dance floor. Studio 54 was the party with no limits at least for the time being.

And it couldn't have happened at a more opportune moment. That same year the soundtrack to the movie "Saturday Night Fever" sold 30 million copies (the highest number for an album up to that time) representing the peak of the disco craze with The Bee Gees' hits "How Deep Is Your Love" and "Stayin' Alive".

Other power albums included "Rumours" (Fleetwood Mac) which hogged the #1 spot for 31 weeks producing the hits "Go Your Own Way", "Dreams", "Don't Stop" and "You Make Lovin' Fun"; "Hotel California" (The Eagles) debunking the west coast mindset with hits such as "New Kid In Town" and "Life In The Fast Lane"; "Aja" (Steely Dan) featuring their funky new jazz sound on "Peg", "Deacon Blues" and "Josie"; and "Songs In the Key Of Life" (Stevie Wonder) with life affirming tracks including "Sir Duke" and "Isn't She Lovely".

It was the year Queen invented the "concept single" "We Will Rock You" backed with "We Are The Champions", two separate sides always played as one continuous performance by radio stations nationwide, an event totally new to music. When professional basketball adopted the hit as a rallying cry, it became the third rock & roll sports anthem.

"Nobody Does It Better" (Carly Simon) sprang from the James Bond film "The Spy Who Loved Me" to a soundtrack for sports coverage, or the best song that ever happened to the male ego. It was also part of the mellow rock format which debuted that year with hits like "Just

The Way You Are" (Billy Joel), "On And On" (Stephan Bishop), "Margaritaville" (Jimmy Buffett), "We're All Alone" (Rita Collidge), "You Light Up My Life" (Debby Boone), and the #1 hit on the Billboard Pop Chart for 1977, "Tonight's The Night Gonna Be Alright" (Rod Stewart).

Among the undercurrents was the increasing use of videos. Queen and Rod Stewart had been filming them for years. 1977 witnessed two video landmarks – Alice Cooper posing as a film noir detective in "You And Me" and the Blue Oyster Cult video "Godzilla" featuring a parade of moments from Japanese sci-fi.

During 1977, the New York City punk club CBGB's witnessed performances by The Ramones, Blondie and The Talking Heads. This with the debut albums by The Clash, Elvis Costello and The Talking Heads were indicators of what was to follow.

Other high points for the year included The Steve Miller Band ("Swingtown"), Donna Summer ("I Feel Love"), Heart ("Barracuda") and Supertramp ("Give A Little Bit").

1978

All of the top five positions on the Billboard Pop Chart on March 4, 1978 were hits written by The Bee Gees: 1) "Stayin' Alive", 2) "How Deep Is Your Love", 3) "Night Fever" (all three sung by The Bee Gees), 4) "Love Is Thicker Than Water (Andy Gibb), 5) "Emotion" (Samantha Sang). This was the only time in history that the same songwriters had a lock on the top five positions. The Bee Gees' younger brother, Andy Gibb, also had the #1 hit on the Billboard Pop Chart for 1978, "Shadow Dancing".

Just as The Bee Gees adapted to disco, other longtime act followed suit including Rod Stewart ("Da Ya Think I'm Sexy"") and The Rolling Stones ("Miss You"). "I Will Survive" (Gloria Gaynor) was the rare disco song with a social message and the greatest anthem to women's empowerment since "Respect", while "Le Freak" (Chic) was inspired by an unsuccessful attempt by group members to enter Studio 54.

Studio 54 was now the most famous party address in the world, but the same publicity that fueled its success now contributed to its downfall. Steve Rubell told New York Magazine, "The profits are astronomical. Only the Mafia does better." This didn't gel with the $7,000 in income taxes paid during 1977. On December 14, IRS agents raided the club, seizing cocaine and a second set of books secreted in the ceiling panels. A lengthy litigation followed lasting more than a year.

High drama became its own musical form when Akron, Ohio band Devo (shorthand for de-evolution) married the basic chord structure of punk to the Euro-synthesizer sound of groups like Kraftwerk to create a nightmare piece of stagecraft where a totalitarian regime seeks to enslave the world with the credo: "Duty Now For The Future!", reinterpreting the Rolling Stones' standard "(I Can't Get No) Satisfaction" for a totally different purpose. It was all part of the cult film "The Truth About De-Evolution" which landed the group on "Saturday Night Live" and other shows.

The album "Bat Out Of Hell" (Meat Loaf) continued in a similar vein with "Paradise By The Dashboard Light" in which a teenage boy and girl debate the meaning of their sexual encounter, while the album "From The Inside" (Alice Cooper) presented life in a mental institution with the crossroads hit "How You Gonna See Me Now".

1978 witnessed Eddie Van Halen pioneering "wanking" on his finger-burning performance "Eruption"; the Bruce Springsteen song "Fire" (The Pointer Sisters); "My Life (Billy Joel); the movie "FM" depicting a rock & roll radio station under siege, and the CBS TV series "WKRP In Cincinnati".

As the decade wound down, the rock audience fled to FM to hear music in true stereo leaving AM radio to the domain of all news formats, talk shows, sporting events and religious broadcasters. With must deserting AM, several former deejays including Don Imus of WLS in Chicago and Rush Limbaugh of KUDL, Kansas City became power players in the switch from music to talk.

The "canned format" programmed by companies thousands of miles away usurped local autonomy, relegating the "disc jockey" to feeding oversized reels of pre-programmed tapes into an automated system where vinyl hadn't been played on the air in years.

1979

"My Sharon" (The Knack), the top hit on the Billboard Pop Chart for 1979, re-energized radio in a way not witnessed since the arrival of The Beatles, helping to ignite one of the greatest summers for rock & roll with hits that included "Bad Case Of Loving You (Doctor Doctor)" (Robert Palmer), "Let's Go" (The Cars), "Don't Bring Me Down" (Electric Light Orchestra), "Girl Of My Dreams" (Bram Tchaikovsky), "Old Time Rock & Roll" (Bob Seger), "Cruel To Be Kind" (Nick Lowe), "Boom Boom Out Go The Lights" (The Pat Travers Band), "Hit Me With Your Rhythm Stick" (Ian Dury & The Blockheads) and the Supertramp album "Breakfast In America" featuring the hits "Goodbye Stranger", "The Logical Song" and "Take The Long Way Home".

Radio began to reflect a veritable supermarket of styles. Blondie fused disco to new wave with "Heart Of Glass". Queen drew from an English rockabilly revival for "Crazy Little Thing Called Love". The Charlie Daniels Band had the hip country crossover "The Devil Went Down To Georgia". Soul music escaped the throes of disco with "After The Love Is Gone" (Earth, Wind & Fire) and Thom Bell's smooth production of "Mama Can't Buy You Love" (Elton John). Bob Dylan went gospel with "Gotta Serve Somebody". The Doobie Brothers effected a touch of jazz in "What A Fool Believes". Kiss planted one foot in heavy metal, the other in disco for "I Was Made For Lovin' You". Styx tapped the romantic vein with "Babe". And disco began to subside, but not before "We Are Family" (Sister Sledge), "Cook With Fire" (Amil Stewart) and "Y.M.C.A." (The Village People).

Events were occurring at a dizzying pace. Digital recording techniques introduced on the album "Bop Til You Drop" (Ry Cooder) led to the development of compact discs during the 1980s. The first music videos were released for sale – "Devo Vision" (Devo) and "Eat To The Beat" (Blondie), a moment dramatized that summer by the hit "Video Killed The Radio Star" (The Buggles), a song that could take its own place in history during 1981.

On the Billboard Album Chart, Led Zepplin's first album in three years, "In Through The Out Door", resulted in the return of all 11 of their previous albums to the Chart, the most complete comeback ever! It was also the year that Fleetwood Mac invested $1 million in their album "Tusk" and the Eagles disbanded after their LP "The Long Run".

Breakthroughs included John Cougar ("I Need A Lover"), Rupert Holmes ("Escape – The Piña Colada Song"), Dan Fogelberg ("Longer") and Chris Thompson & Night ("If You Remember Me"), yet little attention was paid to Chuck Berry's last studio album with original material, "Rockit", featuring one final standard with the single "Oh What A Thrill".

Months of media buildup failed to launch the Japanese duo Pink Lady in the U.S., their single "Kiss In The Dark" spending two weeks in the Top Forty.

Two events closed the decade on a tumultuous note. When Chicago disc jockey Steve Dahl attempted symbolically to bury disco music during pre-game festivities at Comiskey Park, devotees stormed the field causing $1 million in damages and cancellation of the evening's baseball game. More tragically, on December 3 at a concert by The Who in Cincinnati, 11 people were trampled to death. Festival seating – first come, first served – was banned in Cincinnati shortly afterward.

1980

John Lennon had taken a five-year hiatus from music to devote more time to his family. So it was with great anticipation that the public awaited the release of his new album with Yoko Ono, "Double Fantasy", detailing their breakup, subsequent reunion and the purpose that he had discovered in his role as father/househusband.

The single "(Just Like) Starting Over", a triumphant renewal of the couple's vows, had already reached #1 Pop when Lennon was shot to death by a delusional fan outside his New York City apartment house on December 8, 1980. He was 40 years old. Compounding the loss was a sense that Lennon had finally discovered a purpose to life which he was attempting to communicate to others.

In other ways, the 1980s arrived like a jolt to our sensibilities. The in-your-face tone of hits like "Hit Me With Your Best Shot" (Pat Benatar) and "Another One Bites The Dust" (Queen) established a confrontational tone that pervaded the decade. Black music underwent its own transformation during January, 1980 when "Rapper's Delight" (The Sugar Hill Mob) became the first rap hit to reach the Billboard Pop Chart, followed weeks later by "The Breaks" (Kurtis Blow) which reflected greater social relevance.

That same year, the children's cable TV network Nickelodeon began the first television program devoted to music videos, "Popclips". Hosted by comedian Howie Mandel and produced by ex-Monkee Michael Nesmith, it popularized videos like "Brass In Pocket" (The Pretenders) about the secret romantic longings of a waitress.

1980 signaled the full-scale arrival of Bruce Springsteen with the double album "The River" featuring rockers such as "Ramrod" and "Cadillac Ranch" contrasted to bittersweet folk music as "Wreck On The Highway" and sentimental tracks like "I Wanna Marry You". It was also the year that punk spun off into new wave with "Cars" (Gary Numan) and "Clones (We're All)" (Alice Cooper) while The Romantics celebrated the bar band sound in "What I Like About You".

Already there were signs that it wasn't the 70s anymore. Donna Summer's lawsuit over control of her career resulted in the ouster of Neil Bogart at Casablanca Records. Bogart bounced back months later with his new label Boardwalk Entertainment and modest hits like "Together" (Tierra) and "Sequel" (Harry Chapin).

Another 70s icon, Studio 54, closed its doors for fifteen months following the imprisonment of co-owners Steve Rubell and Ian Schrager for income tax evasion. A combination of a new conservative owner, changing musical tastes and the AIDs scare hastened the club's final demise in the mid-80s. Rubell died of complications from AIDs in 1989.

1980 will also be remembered for "Call Me" (Blondie), the #1 hit on the Billboard Pop Chart for 1980; John Travolta trading in the white polyester disco wear for the mechanical bull at Gilley's in the movie "Urban Cowboy"; "I Don't Like Mondays" (The Boomtown Rats) based on a shooting incident in a San Diego schoolyard; "Upside Down" (Diana Ross); "Turning Japanese" (The Vapors); "Same Auld Lang Syne" (Dan Fogelberg); "Teacher Teacher" (Rockpile); "She's Out Of My Life"

(Michael Jackson) – the song in which he continually broke into tears while recording; and the digital vinyl series "Original Master Recordings", the biggest dud since Quad in the search for higher sound quality. If it's a disappointment to drop the needle and nick a $6 album, imagine the feeling when you do it to one costing $20-$25.

Freddie Downs

SHAKEOUT # 4

MUSIC TO WATCH AND FEEL

1981-1990

For more than a decade the culture had been anticipating the next major turnaround act like Elvis or The Beatles. Instead, the change was technology driven. The spread of cable TV and home video recorders resulted in the birth of MTV on August 1, 1981, popularizing music videos, rap, Madonna, the bestselling album of all time, "Thriller" (Michael Jackson), hair bands such as Motley Crue or Def Leppard and CDs (compact discs) which replaced vinyl in less than six years. Shunted onto the oldies shelf were The Eagles, Fleetwood Mac and disco, while music shifted away from the AM band to FM.

The visual image of music videos frequently became more important than the song itself. A hit could have one meaning on the radio and quite another in a video. So MTV and VH-1 challenged radio for breaking new music much in the way that television originally took network radio's audience away during the early 1950s.

The worldwide power of cable TV and satellite transmission carried this video culture beyond political and sociological boundaries. It became a philanthropy movement to combat the Ethiopian famine with "Do They Know It's Christmas?" (Band-Aid) in 1984 and the "Live-

Aid" concert the following year. It also underlined the humanity of European people tasting their freedom with the fall of the Berlin Wall and videos that celebrated the achievement including "Right Here Right Now" (Jesus Jones) and "Winds Of Change" (The Scorpions) and sent a word of comfort to American troops massing for Operation Desert Storm in late 1990 with "Get Here" (Oleta Adams) and "Show Me The Way" (Styx). Songs that made us watch and feel what was transpiring in the world around us.

1981

Inspired by the music video series "Popclips" on Nickelodeon, Robert Pittman, Chief Operating Officer for Warner-Amex Satellite Entertainment, devised the first TV network that could be programmed like a radio station. At 12:00 midnight (EST) on August 1, 1981, it took to the air with a one-minute film of a rocket warming for takeoff.

As the rocket made its dramatic ascent so did the network with the words of an unseen announcer: "Ladies and gentlemen, rock & roll!: Following the image of an astronaut planting a flag on the moon bearing the logo "MTV", the scene segued to the first music video ever played on the network, that prophetic 1979 chestnut "Video Killed The Radio Star" (The Buggles).

Like all great moments in rock & roll, MTV (Music Television) began in the underground. It was emanating from the east coast, but much of the east coast wasn't plugged in. Remote areas of the Midwest could view it, while there was no cable outlet carrying it in New York City and many other major markets.

Its modest library of 250 music videos, 30 of them from Rod Stewart, dated back many years. Only two songs in the Billboard Hot 100 that week had companion videos. Fortunately, the concept was recognized for its potential by emerging acts like Joan Jett and a variety of English bands that fought the uphill battle to convince their record companies of the value of videos now that there was an outlet.

The human face of MTV, its five original VJs (video jocks) were instrumental in establishing the network's image – Martha Quinn, J.J. Jackson, Alan Hunter, Mark Goodman and Nina Blackwood (who doubled as a music reporter for "Entertainment Tonight"). Also important in those early days was the promotional campaign; "I want my MTV!" spoken in ads by Pete Townshend, Pat Benatar, David Bowie and Billy Idol. Those four words helped to create a market.

The 1980s would prove to be an amazing decade technologically with the spread of cable TV, VCRs, home computers and compact discs. What Elvis Presley was to the 1950s and The Beatles to the 1960s, MTV was to the 1980s—rock & roll's first revolution based not on personality or style but rather, technology. A slender thread of film passing through the television that had always been there.

Even before MTV, the 1980s were shaping up as a decade of more selectivity. Few people were athletically inclined to break dance, and many more were frightened away from dance clubs by the first mention of AIDs in

1981. Radio's canned formats and tight playlists were failing to reflect the whole picture, while some artists went too far to stand out, most notably Ozzy Osbourne who bit the head off a live dove during a May, 1981 conference with Epic Records executives. If the old way of business wasn't working anymore, a weary generation would turn somewhere else, making the timing perfect for MTV and the cable TV explosion of the 1980s.

1981would also be remembered for "Bette Davis Eyes" (Kim Carnes), the #1 hit on the Billboard Pop Chart for 1981; "Kiss On My List" and "You Make My Dreams" (Darryl Hall and John Oates); Journey's "Escape" LP featuring "Who's Sorry Now" and "Open Arms"; "Every Little Thing She Does Is Magic" (The Police); "Jessie's Girl" (Rick Springfield); "While You See A Chance" (Steve Winwood); and a reunion of the three surviving Beatles for the tribute to John Lennon's life "All Those Years Ago" (George Harrison).

The Alan Parsons Project seemed to walk a surreal seashore in their 1981 hit "Time" still trying to connect with people and events on Earth from some loftier perch. Along with the 1991 hit "I'll Be There" (The Escape Club), these became two of the most widely used songs at funerals.

1982

MTV demonstrated its power to break English acts who couldn't otherwise gain airplay in the U.S. including Billy Idol ("Hot In The City"), Human League ("Don't You Want Me") and Duran Duran ("Hungry Like The Wolf").

But the success wasn't without controversy. Earth, Wind
& Fire leveled a lawsuit against the network charging that it
didn't play black artists. At year's end when MTV passed
on the video "Billie Jean" (Michael Jackson), it set up a
confrontation with one of America's largest record
conglomerates.

The switchblade sharp motorcycle mean sound of
Joan Jett & The Blackhearts propelled "I Love Rock &
Roll" to #1 Pop, followed months later by the primal "Do
You Wanna Touch Me", a video in which Joan poked her
finger into the camera as if to say 'don't try it, don't even
think it'. One of the few 80s acts not to sell out by
licensing her songs to commercials, Joan relished her role
as the decade's prime badass while bringing The Boardwalk
label its greatest success only weeks prior to Neil Bogart's
death.

George Thorogood & The Destroyers fed off a
similar style with a touch of blues for "Bad To The Bone"
which became the sports anthem for professional wrestlers
and boxers, ending up as the theme for a "Miami Vice"
episode that used the song generously. Like Joan Jett,
Thorogood broke through after years on the concert circuit
with the exposure from MTV.

It was a year of diverse styles and voices – the rap
standard "The Message" (Grand Master Flash & The
Furious Five) which would serve as the underpinning for
90s rap hits by Ice Cube and Puff Daddy; the funk of The
Gap Band ("You Dropped A Bomb On Me"); rockabilly
revisited with The Stray Cats ("Rock This Town"); the
bouncy eco statement "I.G.Y." (Donald Fagan);
"Allentown" (Billy Joel) capturing the desperate economic

times; "Pac Man Fever" (Buckner & Garcia) relating to video game mania; and two more tributes to John Lennon – "Empty Garden" (Elton John) and "Here Today" (Paul McCartney).

In New York City, 22-year-old Madonna Ciccone fashioned a demo tape of her song "Everybody" and convinced deejay Mark Kamins to play it at the fashionable club Danceteria. Its popularity convinced Sire Records to release the song as a 12-inch dance single during April, 1982. A hit on the Billboard Dance Chart, it introduced the woman who would finish the decade an icon.

Other highlights included the #1 hit on the Billboard Pop Chart for 1982 "Physical" (Olivia Newton-John); "Rock The Casbah" (The Clash); "I'm So Excited" (The Pointer Sisters); the Kentucky Derby sports anthem "Run For The Roses" (Dan Fogelberg); "Hurts So Good" (John Cougar); "Eye In The Sky" (The Alan Parsons Project); "Gypsy" (Fleetwood Mac); "Cynical Girl" (Marshall Crenshaw); and "Abracadabra" (The Steve Miller Band).

Ozzy Osbourne was banned in Boston after a Des Moines, Iowa concert in 1982 where he bit the head off a live bat, believing it to be a rubber bat provided for the stunt. As a precaution, he underwent a rabies vaccination following the concert.

1983

Even after "Billie Jean" became a major hit on the Pop Chart, MTV refused to play the video viewing Michael Jackson as an artist who appealed mainly to black audiences. Discreetly, Columbia Records gave MTV an ultimatum to either air the next Jackson video "Beat It" or suffer an embargo from Columbia and its associated labels.

"Beat It" made the rotation and gradually a higher percentage of black artists such as Run DMC and Eddy Grant followed. 1983 was Michael's peak year. The LP "Thriller" which both hits were from spent 37 weeks at #1 generating 7 Top Forty hits and selling 47 million copies, the bestselling album of all time.

At this same time, Michael made history as a dancer. While singing "Billie Jean" at Motown's 25th Anniversary Television Special on March 23, Michael introduced the moonwalk, a radical step that created the illusion of walking in reverse.

On December 2, 1983, MTV premiered the lavish 13-minute video "Thriller" directed by John Landis. The first video to cost a million dollars to produce, it featured Michael's transformation into both a werewolf and a zombie, but the most memorable effect was the dancing, particularly the zombie street dance where Michael balanced on his toes in classic ballet style. "Thriller" served notice that videos were more than just commercials to sell records. At their best, they were movies in their own right.

Practically overshadowed by the "Thriller" hype was the introduction of the first compact discs. Developed in Europe by the Phillips and Polygram labels, the CD required its own unique playback system, but surprisingly the public took to the idea in less than five years.

At this same time, the first strains of 80s "hair metal" thundered in with the albums "Shout At The Devil"

(Motley Crue) and "Pyromania" (Def Leppard). The latter sold 7 million copies thanks to hits such as "Photograph" and "Rock Of Ages", signaling a trend toward big 80s hair, self-indulgence, raunchiness and scantily clad women.

The synthesizer sound was hot on hits like "Sweet Dreams (Are Made Of This)" (The Eurythmics) and "She Blinded Me With Science" (Thomas Dolby) while the term "new music" became an all encompassing phrase for emerging acts that broke with the past such as Oxo ("Whirly Girl"), After The Fire ("Der Komissar"), Madness ("Our House"), Spandau Ballet ("True") and The Motels ("Suddenly Last Summer").

A new trend debuted in the New York City dance clubs when DJ John "Jellybean" Benitez created his own remix of established hits by adding an independently-produced bass line or rhythm section that would take the song into deeper dance territory. Crowds flocked to Jellybean's appearances at Studio 54, Xenon and The Fun House to hear his new take on familiar hits. In time, record companies would release multiple variations of the same song.

Aspiring singer Madonna Ciccone asked Jellybean to put his touch to her demo tape "Holiday" and the song became her first hit on the Billboard Pop Chart during October, 1983.

Commercial milestones for the year included the LP "An Innocent Man" (Billy Joel) reflecting on a wide variety of music from the 50s and 60s and "Eliminator" (Z Z Top) featuring the rock classics "Legs" and "Sharp Dressed Man", songs taken to a new level in music videos where three magical women make a dream come true for some downtrodden character.

On July 21, 1983, Diana Ross braved 50mph winds and an unrelenting downpour in her concert in Central Park, proving that she owned the stage that night, not the weather.

Another longstanding icon, Todd Rundgren, released "Bang The Drum All Day" which initially stiffed, only to be rediscovered during the mid to late 90s in a series of movies and television commercials that utilized the song to exemplify the party atmosphere of weekends.

Among the year's other highlights – the #1 hit on the Billboard Pop Chart for 1983 "Every Breath You Take" (The Police); "One Thing Leads to Another" (The Fixx); "Pink Houses" (John Cougar); "That's All" (Genesis); "Delirious" (Prince); "The Safety Dance" (Men Without Hats); "The Curly Shuffle" (Jump N' The Saddle), a novelty dance based on The Three Stooges; and "Solitaire" (Laura Brannigan), the breakthrough hit for songwriter Diane Warren whose work greatly defined the 80s and 90s.

"I Melt With You" (Modern English) would quickly become one of the most frequently used hits in a variety of coming of age movies during the 1980s.

1984

In England, Bob Geldof, lead singer of The Boomtown Rats, was so emotionally moved by television coverage of the Ethiopian famine that he decided to get involved by organizing Band-Aid, a one-time gathering of English and American performers for the cause.

Banarama, Culture Club, Phil Collins, Duran Duran, Frankie Goes To Hollywood, Heaven 17, Kool & The Gang, Paul McCartney, Spandau Ballet, Status Quo, Sting, The Style Council, Ultravox, U2, Jodi Watley, Wham! And Paul Young combined their voices for the singles hit "Do They Know It's Christmas?" which raised $11 million and sparked an even greater commitment worldwide during 1985.

With its seven hits, "Born In The U.S.A." (Bruce Springstein) dominated the year like no other album, the title cut serving as a laundry list for what was wrong with the country, as well as a statement of patriotism in spite of it. Springsteen threw so much power into the vocal that his fans worried he might destroy his voice, but "The Boss" showed no sign of letting up whether contrasting the skill of baseball to the artistry of a bar band in the video "Glory Days" or pulling on overwhelmed fan (Courtney Cox) from the audience to boogie on stage in the video "Dancing In The Dark".

With the videos "Burning Up", "Lucky Star" and "Borderline", Madonna arrived at MTV drawing immediate attention with her haphazard wardrobe, bare midriff, "boy toy" belt and a legion of identically dressed fans, "the wannabees". Her breakthrough paralleled that of Cyndi Lauper ("Girls Just Want To Have Fun"). Lauper had the more commanding voice, but was quickly outdistanced by Madonna who excelled in marketing herself.

The year's most unexpected sensation, 45-year-old

Tina Turner, bounded back into the spotlight with the album "Private Dancer" which spawned five hits, most notably "What's Love Got To Do With It". With the famous stage strut that Mick Jagger had borrowed, the gruff/smokey vocals, wild hair and the most perfect legs in show business, Tina Turner covered a stage like no one else.

Michael Jackson continued his phenomenal success. His duet with Paul McCartney, "Say Say Say", was the #1 hit on the Billboard Pop Chart for 1984 and McCartney's fourth with that honor, an unprecedented feat. Michael's video "The Making of Thriller" was the first to sell a million copies, while The Jackson's video "Torture" introduced choreographer Paula Abdul, a former L.A. Laker's cheerleader who would go on to work even greater music video magic during the next few years with Janet Jackson, Z Z Top, Steve Winwood and George Michael before taking the spotlight on her own.

Other standout moments for 1984 included the generation gap anthem of the decade "When Doves Cry" (Prince); Twisted Sister's statement of headbanger resolve "We're Not Gonna Take It"; The Car's whimsical video "You Might Think"; English comedienne Tracy Ullman's sole hit "They Don't Know"; and former Creedance Clearwater Revival frontman John Fogerty's comeback hit "The Old Man Down The Road" which spawned a lawsuit from his previous record label for sounding similar to the CCR hit "Run Through The Jungle", also written by Fogerty. In court Fogerty was judged innocent of plagiarizing himself.

1985

The seasonal success of "Do They Know Its Christmas?" prompted the American music community to ask how they could get involved in the Ethiopian famine relief effort. Michael Jackson and record producer Quincy Jones got the ball rolling by assembling 42 of the top names in music for America's answer record "We Are The World".

On January 28, 1985 at A&M Records in Los Angeles, they gathered for a session which lasted from midnight to sunrise, a legendary ensemble which included Bruce Springsteen, Cyndi Lauper, Stevie Wonder, Diana Ross, The Pointer Sisters, Huey Lewis, Tina Turner, Billy Joel, Paul Simon, Bob Dylan, Ray Charles and Journey's Steve Perry, among others.

"We Are The World" (USA For Africa) reached #1 on the Billboard Pop Chart garnering $40 million for famine relief. It united England and America for the next phase of the effort, the 16-hour "Live Aid Concert" (July 13) originating primarily from two stadiums – JFK in Philadelphia and Wembley in London with additional cut-ins from Russia, Australia and other points.

$140 million was raised by the concert which featured 60 acts including Mick Jagger and Tina Turner, Madonna, The Who, The Cars, Eric Clapton, Elton John, Boy Dylan, Paul Young and Phil Collins (who performed separate sets hours apart at both JFK and Wembley). The group Queen gave a landmark performance. The Band Aid Trust, sponsors of Live Aid, would continue its philanthropy work into the 21st century.

From here the philanthropy movement splintered into a dozen causes including "Farm Aid" concerts to help family farmers and the angry single "Sun City" (Artists United Against Apartheid) addressing South Africa's segregationist society.

Apart from social causes, music flared in other directions. "Brother In Arms" (Dire Straits) was the year's influential album with a touch of jazz ("Your Latest Trick"), country ("So Far Away") and spacey lullaby ("Why Worry"). But the standout track "Money For Nothing", the world's first CD single and a broadside at the whole video culture, became a huge hit and the unofficial theme of MTV.

"Walk Of Life", the album's second single, was transferred to video as a series of action shots from professional football and basketball games. A similar direction occurred with "Centerfield" (John Fogerty) which drew its video imagery from film footage of baseball greats Babe Ruth, Willie Mays and Joe DiMaggio. Baseball parks everywhere began blasting the song through their public address systems making it the sports anthem for baseball.

Still, the biggest star in videos was Madonna who utilized the genre to communicate a social message. Her identity piece, "Material Girl", revealed the gap between reality and the public perception of celebrities.

1985 was the year VH-1 debuted, a second music video network from MTV aimed at a more mature audience. Marvin Gaye's performance of "The Star Spangled Banner" from the 1982 All Star Game in Los Angeles was the video used to launch the network.

Legendary Chicago deejay Don Imus was the first VH-1 VJ.

1985 was also the year of U.S. Senate hearings into obscene lyrics featuring testimony from Twisted Sister's Dee Snider, 60s underground star Frank Zappa and folkie John Denver. Rick Nelson, 45, died in a fiery plane crash while en route to a concert. And "Walk Thru Rock", a traveling museum of vintage rock & roll film clips, made its way through selected cities.

Among other highlights: The #1 hot on the Billboard Pop Chart for 1985, "Careless Whisper (Wham!); "Summer of '69"(Bryan Adams); "The Search Is Over" (Survivor); "Everybody Wants To Rule The World" (Tears For Fears); "We Built This City" (Starship); "Everytime You Go Away" (Paul Young); and "Rhythm Of The Night (DeBarge) written by Diane Warren.

1986

Sooner or later rap and rock would blend. "Walk This Way" (Run DMC) was that historic moment in 1986. Originally a popular 1976 single by Aerosmith, this version laid a rap rhythm over the famous Joe Perry guitar solo. Steven Tyler and Joe Perry of Aerosmith both participated in the single and video. In the latter, the forces of rap and rock seem to be trying to outdo one another. In reality, the hit arrived at a low ebb for Aerosmith, setting them up for over a decade of major hits and popular music videos.

At MTV, the first major shakeout occurred. The network acquired Rolling Stone journalist Kurt Loder to establish a news division separate from music programming. Feeling slighted over losing their news and interview duties, Nina Blackwood and J.J. Jackson departed the network followed weeks later by the other three original VJs. A new staff was put in place, including the unpredictable Downtown Julie Brown whose well displayed figure and catch phrase "wubba wubba wubba" guided MTV through a more sexually provocative era.

At this point, it was almost impossible to have a hit record without a video and 1986 offered a bumper crop; "Sledgehammer (Peter Gabriel), a landmark of start/stop clay animation; "Land Of Confusion" (Genesis) featuring marionette likenesses of every major figure from the Reagan era; "Addicted To Love" (Robert Palmer) with its expressionless robot women; "Take On Me" (a ha) where a beautiful woman is drawn into a dangerous cartoon universe; "Missionary Man" (The Eurythmics) featuring zipper overkill and Annie Lennox prancing around like a leather clad Frankenstein.

A different wrinkle found Madonna teaming with MTV for the "Make My Video Contest" resulting in a primitive black and white rendering of teenage life which became "True Blue".

Videos like "The Pleasure Principle" where Janet Jackson worked alone with limited props and the most basic dance steps as a dancer can perform helped Janet to emerge from the shadow of her famous brother. For more than a year Janet sharpened her dance skills under the special tutoring of Paula Abdul who choreographed Janet's videos "Nasty" and "Control".

1986 was the year of the Genesis album "Invisible Touch" with hits like "In Too Deep" and "Throwing It All Away"; Latino sensations Gloria Estefan and The Miami Sound Machine ("Words Get In The Way"); The Bangles ("Manic Monday"); "At This Moment" (Billy Vera & The Beaters) which shot to #1 after being featured in a romantic dance sequence between Michael J. Fox and Tracy Pollen on the sitcom "Family Ties"; "What You Need" (INXS); "Sweet Love" (Anita Baker); and "Keep Your Hands To Yourself" (The Georgia Satellites).

Capitol Records staged the successful comeback of Heart ("These Dreams") while Paul Simon's "Graceland" album combined New York City street smarts with the rhythms and vocals of Africa on hits like "Diamonds On The Souls Of His Shoes", a foray into world music. Even the #1 hit on the Billboard Pop Chart for 1986 brought together four music legends. "That's What Friends Are For" (Dionne & Friends) was a quartet comprised of Dionne Warwick, Stevie Wonder, Gladys Knight and Elton John. Proceeds from the hit went to AIDs research.

1987

Metal "hair bands" were hot, typified by the mile high hair and makeup overkill of Poisen ("Talk Dirty To Me") and the abundance of gorgeous uninhibited women like actress Tawny Kitean hanging out the window of the speeding car in the video "Here I Go Again" (Whitesnake). The lifestyle of booze, drugs, sex and merciless amplification was dramatized in the video "Home Sweet Home" (Motley Crue) and put into practice by most of the individuals playing the music.

The Def Leppard album "Hysteria" sold 11 million copies sending hits up the Chart such as "Armageddon It" and "Pour Some Sugar On Me". Their first album in four years, it represented a triumph over adversity for drummer Rick Allen who lost his left arm in a car crash during 1984. With an electric drum set that he played with his feet, Allen became a source of inspiration for millions of fans.

1987 was the breakout year for REM with their fifth album, "Document", featuring the hits "It's The End Of The World As We Know It (And I Feel Fine)" and the frequently misread ballad "The One I Love" which was intended as sarcasm but somehow widely misinterpreted as a statement of undying love. REM continually thanked college radio for sustaining their music during the lean years.

It was the year of the avant-garde single "Need You Tonight/Mediate" by INXS from the landmark album "Kick" which also featured the hits "Devil Inside" and "New Sensation"; the first cassette single "Heat Of The Night" (Bryan Adams); and the Yellow song "Oh Yeah", making its way from Twix candy commercials to a variety of applications in TV and movies.

Former Wham! heartthrob George Michael struck the 80s rebel pose in his black leather jacket with foot perched against a juke box in the video "Faith". Songwriter Diane Warren continued her winning ways penning "Love Will Lead You Back" (Taylor Dane), "I Get Weak" (Belinda Carlisle), and the #1 smash "Nothing's Gonna Stop Us Now" (Starship) from the movie "Mannequin".

Other films that made an impact included "Dirty Dancing" starring Patrick Swayze, featuring the #1 smash "Hungry Eyes" (Eric Carmen), and "Light Of Day" starring Joan Jett and Michael J. Fox in a bleak portrayal of the bar band circuit.

After several critically acclaimed movie roles, Cher redefined herself as an actress with three major films in 1987 – "Moonstruck", "Suspect", and "The Witches Of Eastwick".

The year will also be remembered for "Walk Like An Egyptian" (The Bangles), the #1 hit on the Billboard Pop Chart for 1987; "I Still Haven't Found What I'm Looking For" (U2); the wedding standard "Always" (Atlantic Starr); "I Wanna Dance With Somebody" (Whitney Houston); "Looking For A New Love" (Jody Watley); "Smokin' Gun" (The Robert Cray Band); The Grateful Dead's only music video, "Touch Of Grey"; and former Beatle George Harrison reaching a moment of MTV stardom with the video "Got My Mind Set On You".

1988

A carryover from 1987, "Faith" (George Michael) became the #1 hit on the Billboard Pop Chart for 1988, while the "Faith" album continued to flood the Chart with hits including "Father Figure" and the jazz ballad "Kissing A Fool".

1988 was the year Guns N' Roses debuted with the LP "Appetite For Destruction" featuring the hits "Sweet Child O'Mine" and "Paradise City". Their manic hit

"Welcome To The Jungle" captured the maddening din of contemporary life, while the thoughtful follow-up "Patience" seemed to suggest the solution. Lead singer Axl Rose quickly became the most celebrated rock screamer since Led Zeppelin's Robert Plant.

The songwriting duo of Antonio "L.A." Reid and Kenny "Babyface" Edmonds found first success penning the hits "Don't Be Cruel" (Bobby Brown), "The Lover In Me" (Sheena Easton) and Paula Abdul's first single "Knocked Out". Edmonds and Reid would become the prime songwriting power of the 90s.

It was the year of "new jack swing", exemplified by "My Prerogative" (Bobby Brown); the first 900 fanline pioneered by the rap duo DJ Jazzy Jeff & The Fresh Prince after their generation gap hit "Parents Just Don't Understand"; Tracy Chapman's savvy survival ballad "Fast Car"; and the headbanger classic "I Hate Myself For Loving You" (Joan Jett & The Blackhearts) that struck a universal nerve with anyone who ever tried to break free from a relationship that was taking more of a negative toll than it was worth.

Several music videos made powerful statements including "Fallen Angel" (Poison) about Hollywood's user mentality and "Beds Are Burning" (Midnight Oil) which took up the plight of Australia's Aboriginal people who were being crowded off their land by greedy developers. From the purely visual standpoint, there was the video "Roll With It" (Steve Winwood) choreographed by Paula Abdul and the return of the robot women from "Addicted To Love" in the video "Simply Irresistible" (Robert Palmer).

The release of the album "Bad" (Michael Jackson), the long anticipated sequel to "Thriller", proved a mixed blessing. After selling 8 million copies and spawning five #1 hits, it was still compared less favorably to its predecessor. Michael's video "Leave Me Alone" was a tour-de-force against the tabloid headlines swirling about him, showing that the personal scars were running deep.

It was also a year for goodbyes. One of the longest running sagas of the rock era came to an end during September when the 1973 album "Dark Side Of The Moon" (Pink Floyd) dropped from the Chart after spending 741 consecutive weeks (a full 15 1/2 years), the longest duration of any album in the history of the Chart. Another longevity act, Casey Kasem, the originator of "American Top 40", left the series after 18 years to host a similar countdown show for a higher salary.

The saddest farewell was the death of Roy Orbison, 52, on December 6 after battling heart disease for more than a decade. His career had been enjoying a resurgence with the solo hit "You Got It" and as a member of The Traveling Wilburys and their singles smash "Handle With Care".

1988 would also be remembered for "Desire" (U2); The Beach Boys' first #1 hit in twenty years, "Kokomo" from the Tom Cruise movie "Cocktail"; "Every Rose Has Its Thorn" (Poisen); "The Wild Wild West" (The Escape Club); "When The Children Cry" (White Lion); and "I Know You're Out There Somewhere" (The Moody Blues).

1989

"Like A Prayer" (Madonna), MTV's top video for 1989, caused a tremendous social stir. The story of a witness to a murder who eventually brings the perpetrators to justice, the video featured religious references such as crosses burning and a church statue coming to life and kissing Madonna. Without first seeing the video, Pepsi Cola based a much ballyhooed commercial around the song, only to shelve it after two airings when the music video drew fire from the Catholic Church. Pepsi cancelled Madonna's contract for future ads, but she kept the $4 million.

A different type of controversy surrounded the dreadlocked European duo Milli Vanilli whose debut album "Girl You Know It's True" garnered three #1 singles and a Grammy for best new artist. Later when it was confirmed that the duo did none of the singing on the record, a Grammy was rescinded for the first time in history and the Arista label provided a $3 refund to an estimated 80,000 consumers.

A breath of fresh air amid the controversy was choreographer Paula Abdul whose album "Forever Your Girl" misfired badly in 1988. The first two singles stiffed, but the third "Straight Up" made her the success story of 1989, dancing her way through subsequent hits "Forever Your Girl", "Cold Hearted", "(It's Just) The Way That You Love Me" and "Opposites Attract".

Abdul's former protégé, Janet Jackson, released "Rhythm Nation", a dance album rife with social commentary about gangs, drug addiction and the importance of education, while Phil Collins addressed the issue of homelessness with "Another Day In Paradise".

As big as any record, the Spike Lee movie "Do The Right Thing" with its jazz and rap soundtrack alternated between the shrill and the surreal to cause a generation to re-examine its racial attitudes.

Music videos made a wide variety of statements as well: "18 & Life" (Skid Row) deglamorized a life of crime; "One" (Metallica) was a riveting anti-war statement; "Rockit" (Def Leppard) a tribute to a quarter century of rock & roll innovators; "Groove Is In The Heart" (Deee Lite), a slice of New York City dance club life; "Veronica" (Elvis Costello), an elegant look at the different stages of a woman's life' "Lost In Your Eyes" (Debbie Gibson), a kindred look at 80s romance; "If I Could Turn Back Time" (Cher), proof that even a woman of 40 can get a battleship in an uproar.

AT the MTV Video Music Awards on September 6, Jon Bon Jovi and Richie Sambora performed an acoustic version of "Wanted Dead Or Alive", inspiring the network to fashion a regular concert series where rock and rap acts would do the same. "MTV Unplugged" debuted November 28 with a concert by The Squeeze.

It was the year that REM ("Stand!") bolted the IRS Label for Warner Brothers while IRS introduced The Fine Young Cannibals ("She Drives Me Crazy"); Young MC gave rap its catch phrase "Bust A Move" and co-wrote the perfect marriage between rock and rap, "Funky Cold Medina" (Tone Loc); disclaimer labels "18 to Purchase" and "Parental Advisory" first appeared on records as a hedge against government regulation; and Kenny "Babyface" Edmonds sang his first hit "It's No Crime" while continuing to provide songs such as "I'm Your Baby

Tonight" (Whitney Houston) and "Every Little Step" (Bobby Brown).

Other highlights included the #1 hit on the Billboard Pop Chart for 1989, "Look Away" (Chicago), written by Diane Warren; the Swedish duo Roxette ("The Look"); "Love Shack" (The B-52s), the homage to a swinging club in the middle of nowhere; "The Living Years" (Mike & The Mechanics); the boom-shacka-lacka-lacka dance craze "Walk The Dinosaur " (Was Not Was); "No Myth" (Michael Penn); and "Don't Want To Fall In Love" Jane Child), best remembered for her spiked hair and a chain running from her nostril to her earlobe.

Dick Clark, the man TV Guide once labeled "the oldest living teenager", stepped down as host to "American Bandstand" after 22 years. The show continued for one more season without him.

1990

"Vogue", a dance craze dating back to the 1920s where dancers assume a position like mannequins, suddenly found a spokeswoman in Madonna whose video by the same name paid tribute to Hollywood's glamorous past while adding a chic fashion sense. The video's debut was momentous enough to warrant a five-minute segment on "The NBC Nightly News."

Her public service announcement for "Rock The Vote" presented Madonna in a red bikini with the American flag draped across her shoulders and the tease line of the year: "And if you don't vote, you're going to get a spanky!"

Critics wondered when she would go too far even for MTV. It happened Saturday, December 1, 1990 when the network refused to air her voyeuristic video "Justify My Love" after more than a week of promotion. Two days later, ABC TVs "Nightline" aired the video uncut and interviewed Madonna. "Justify My Love" was then released as the first video single selling more than 400,000 copies.

The daring sensuality Madonna brought to her work would reflect in the videos of other acts including Paula Abdul and Salt-N-Pepa. When Janet Jackson performed "Black Cat" at the MTV Video Music Awards that September she popped her blouse open and danced around the stage in a black bra, something that would have been unthinkable only a year before.

Besides sex rock & roll entered the new decade with its power intact to outrage evidenced by the chaotic alternative hit "Been Caught Stealing" (Jane's Addiction), a bizarre tribute to the five-finger discount. The commercial breakthrough killed the group. Lead singer Perry Farrell moved on the Porno For Pyros and into a promotional role for The Lollapolooza Tour.

Movies exerted a considerable influence. Christian Slater starred as an underground deejay staying just one step ahead of the law in "Pump Up The Jam". The soundtrack by Technotronic popularized "house music" dance hits like "Get Up (Before The Night Is Over)" and "Move This".

The film "Pretty Woman" made a 90s icon of Julia

Roberts while launching the hits "The King Of Wishful Thinking" (Go West) and "It Must Have Been Love" (Roxette) while unearthing a little known Iggy Pop song "Real Wild Child (Wild One)" (Christopher Otcasek) which soon received a workout on beer commercials.

At year's end with thousands of American military troops massed in Saudi Arabia for Operation Desert Storm, a pair of hits seemed to address the feelings of hope and separation experienced by both the troops in the field and their families back home – "Get Here" (Oleta Adams) and "Show Me The Way" (Styx).

It was the year that the guitar bed to Rick James' 1981 fund hit "Super Freakl" resurfaced in the rap song "U. Can't Touch This" (MC Hammer), MTVs Top Video for 1990; the #1 hit on the Billboard Pop Chart for 1990 "Hold On" (Wilson Phillips) featuring the daughters of The Beach Boys' Brian Wilson and The Mamas & The Papas' John Phillips; "Vision Of Love" (Mariah Carey), her debut hit; the return of Ted Nugent in Damn Yankees ("High Enough"); The Black Crows popularizing a little known Otis Redding song, "Hard To Handle"; the 90s catch phrase for making love, "Knockin Boots" (Candyman); The Rolling Stones 3-D concert on the Fox Network; and the debut of "Beach MTV" with VJ Daisy Fuentes who did a lot for the bikini and the exclamation, "Cool!".

SHAKEOUT # 5

ONE SONG CHANGES EVERYTHING

1991-into the 21ˢᵗ Century

It was a dark music about personal torment and being misunderstood. Nirvana had no delusions of glory or success when they played the Seattle club scene or even when they released their album "Nevermind" in 1991. Within weeks the album had reached #1, sweeping aside former heavy hitters including Michael Jackson and Guns N' Roses. Its hit "Smells Like Teen Spirit" became the rallying cry for Generation X, announcing a new music that broke with the past. It rewrote the definition of a rock star as someone much less than perfect who walks among us. Lead singer Kurt Cobain had never sought fame, and less than four years later the combination of fame, drugs and a shotgun ended his short life. Yet to many in the 90s, the moment and its music were real. And those artists who no longer seemed real – the hair bands of the 80s, Michael Jackson mired in scandals—lost their position of importance.

As MTV and VH-1 de-emphasized music programming, the Internet took up the slack with a series of web sites programming music formats much in the way that AM radio had during the 1950s. CD and cassette singles vanished as the computer download became the new single of choice. Satellite radio became the audio version of cable TV with its myriad of formats. IPods allowed the listener on the go to carry with them their entire record collection on one disc. Cassettes disappeared while the CD and DVD formats became threatened by Blu-Ray.

The most massive homicide on American soil, the terrorist attacks of September 11, 2001 didn't signal the conclusion of this shakeout, but music was an important part of the healing process.

1991

It was supposed to be the autumn of heavy hitters. The two double discs "Use Your Illusion I and II" (Guns N' Roses) featured enough singles to keep the group on the Charts for two years, including MTV's top video for 1991, "You Could Be Mine". The two albums entered the Billboard Chart at #1 and #2 on October 5, retaining theses positions the following week, the same week that an obscure album, "Nevermind" (Nirvana), first appeared at #144.

Michael Jackson returned with "Dangerous", his most important album since "Thriller", including hits like "Heal The World" and "Will You Be There". To launch the album, Jackson's lavish video "Black Or White" debuted November 14 at 8:25 p.m. EST, simulcast on MTV, BET and the Fox network. The album debuted at #1. Each of the successive hits from "Dangerous" were given the same simulcast premiere on multiple networks, the last time that Michael would command such attention. The child molestation charges of the following years eroded his career in America yet he remained extremely popular overseas.

During November, MTV began airing the video "Smells Like Teen Spirit" (Nirvana) described by critics as a pep rally from Hell with its dark, turbulent atmosphere. At that moment, teens and those in their early 20s discovered a music of their own which totally broke with the past. With its minimalistic approach, slacker sensibilities and a lyric that no one over 25 could embrace, let alone comprehend, it became the anthem of rage freaks, bored angry youth blaming their parents for gutting their future and self-absorbed slackers whose sub-par lifestyle was celebrated by the song.

Gone overnight were the 80s hair bands such as Def Leppard and Poisen, replaced by grunge's flannel and denim everyman, oblivious and contemptuous of fame and fortune, making party music of their own pain and angst. "Smells Like Teen Spirit" rewrote the rules of what it was to be a rock star as the album "Nevermind" nudged "Dangerous" out of the #1 position after only one week! Generation X had arrived.

In 1991 two comebacks inspired an entire generation. After suffering two crushed vertebrae in an automobile accident and undergoing a year of rigorous therapy, Gloria Estefan sang about the ordeal in "Coming Out Of The Dark". At the same time, Vanessa Williams crossed over from R&B to the Pop Chart with the sassy dance hit "Runnin' Back To You". Stripped of her Miss America title in 1984 after a scandal involving nude photographs, Vanessa returned to dominate the 90s with hit records, videos, movies, starring roles on the Broadway stage and VJ duties at VH-1.

The fall of Communism in Europe and the dismantling of the Berlin Wall had not only made for history but great music with "Right Here Right Now" (Jesus Jones) and "Winds Of Change" (The Scorpions). 1991 witnessed a return to vocal harmony groups such as Boyz II Men ("It's So Hard To Say Goodbye To Yesterday") and Color Me Badd ("I Adore Me Amore"); philosophical statements of REM ("Losing My Religion") and U2 (Mysterious Ways"); industrial strength dance music of C&C Music Factory ("Gonna Make You Sweat"); power ballads by Extreme ("More Than Words") and Firehouse ("Love Of A Lifetime"); and contemporary Christian artists like Amy Grant ("Baby Baby") and Michael W. Smith ("For You") expanding to secular music.

MTV televised its own birthday party "MTV At 10" featuring Aerosmith, George Michael, REM and Madonna culminating in an extravagant production of "Will You Be There" by Michael Jackson featuring hundreds of singers and dancers and ending with an angel descending from the rafters to wrap Michael protectively in her wings.

Among the other highlights of the year, the #1 song on the Billboard Pop Chart for 1991 "Everything I Do I Do For You" (Bryan Adams) from the Kevin Costner film "Robin Hood"; Metallica's nightmare video "Enter Sandman"; a rap hit for the AIDs era, "Let's Talk About Sex" (Salt-N-Pepa); and I'll Be There" (The Escape Club), a second hit favored at funerals.

It was also the year Nickelodeon presented the teenager of the 90s, "Clarissa Explains It All", starring Melissa Joan Hart looking directly into the camera and addressing the viewer like a friend over for a visit.

With the movie and hit song "Pelo Suelto", Gloria Trevi became an audience magnet for the Spanish language network Univision. In spite of two subsequent albums and two additional movies by 1995, she still couldn't make a big break-through in America. Univision viewers marveled at her climbing furniture or undressing a male audience member while she sang. A cult figure for the 90s.

1992

Thirteen weeks at #1 made "End Of The Road" (Boyz II Men) the #1 hit on the Billboard Pop Chart for 1992. Co-written by Babyface, L.A. Reid and Daryl Simmons, the hit was part of the soundtrack for the Eddie Murphy film "Boomerang" which also featured "I'd Die Without You" (P. M. Dawn), "Love Should Have Brought You Home" (Toni Braxton) and "Pull Up To The Bumper" (Patra).

The popularity of Boyz II Men opened a wider vein for vocal harmony acts including En Vogue ("My Lovin' You're Never Gonna Get It") and Jade ("Don't Walk Away") while LaFace Records, co-owned by Babyface and Reid, released one of the year's hottest rap albums "Ooo...On The TLC Tip" (TLC) which sought to reinforce positive values and individuality in women with hits like What About Your Friends" and the #1 smash, "Baby Baby Baby".

Positive statements became more the exception than the rule. "The Chronic" (Dr. Dre) was the album that caused MTV to add more gangsta rap videos to the rotation with their bleak images of drug deals, shootings, prison life, liquor gulped from paper cups, cars bouncing and hand signs popularized by street gangs. Some hip hop artists boasted of gang affiliations knowing the danger card would play well in white suburbia where conditions were too well ordered.

The street culture portrayed in the music suggested that human life was cheap, women were lower class and laws were meant to be broken. The 1992 Presidential campaign found the candidates debating the social harm of inflammatory rap songs like "Cop Killer" (Ice T.).

While it couldn't equal the sensationalism of gangsta rap, grunge was feeding off the same themes of desperation and violence, whether it was the opening of the video "Come As You Are" (Nirvana) showing a gun floating in the water or "Jeremy" (Pearl Jam) where an awkward kid resorts to violence against bullies.

Offsetting the violence chic was "Tears In Heaven" (Eric Clapton) in which a father mourns the loss of his son with a monologue of unanswered questions. Clapton's son Conner had died in a fall from a high rise apartment during 1991.

Other memorable moments from the year included MTV's Top Video for 1992, "November Rain" (Guns N' Roses); the epic ballad of loneliness and alienation, "Under The Bridge (The Red Hot Chili Peppers); "Save The Best For Last" (Vanessa Williams) where in a woman gently sorts through her husband's infidelity; "Jump Around" (House of Pain), a tribute to the dance known as the pogo where people jump up and down in a stationary motion; and the video "Erotica" (Madonna), a tour-de-force of sex fetish and S&M which MTV ran uncut but only once a night at 12:00 midnight (EST).

1993

1993's most enduring image, the cover of the September 16 issue of Rolling Stone Magazine, featured a shirtless Janet Jackson with two male hands strategically shielding her breasts, an instant sellout which spun off into a CD cover photo and the decade's hottest poster.

It was the year when those who didn't belong drew sustenance from the mood piece "Creep" (Radiohead) and the Nirvana album "In Utero" which savaged the big business that grunge had become. During November when Nirvana performed on "MTV Unplugged", it was mostly an hour of obscure material giving Kurt Cobain a showcase for his tormented vocals. His suicide only five months away, the concert would later take on the connotation of a farewell.

New talent made a profound impact on the year including the Irish group The Cranberries ("Linger"), Sweden's Ace of Base ("All That She Wants"), Sisters With Voices ("Weak"), The Gin Blossoms ("Found Out About You") and Toni Braxton's debut album featuring "Another Sad Love Song", "Breathe Again" and "You Mean The World To Me", songs penned by Babyface, L.A. Reid and Daryl Simmons.

Movie actress Alicia Silverstone saw her career take off after starring in the Aerosmith video "Cryin'", MTV's top video for 1993. Other video landmarks included

"Runaway Train" (Soul Asylum) which took up the plight of missing children and "No Rain" (Blind Melon) concerning a tap dancing bee girl seeking social acceptance.

Television gave us "Bad Boys" (Inner Circle), the theme from the reality based series "Cops", and the soundtrack to "Beverly Hills 90210" featuring the #1 Pop hit "Love Is" (Vanessa Williams & Brian McKnight). Although no one realized it at the time, the new "Mickey Mouse Club" on the Disney Channel was serving as an incubator for new talent with a new generation of Mousketeers that including Britney Spears and future N'Sync members Justin Timberlake and J.C. Chasez.

Movies were having an impact as well. The Kevin Costner film "The Bodyguard" spawned the #1 hit on the Billboard Pop Chart for 1993, "I Will Always Love You" (Whitney Houston), while two little known 80s chestnuts reached the Chart after being featured in cult movies. The Johnny Depp film "Benny & June" launched the 1987 track "I'm Gonna Be – 500 Miles" (The Proclaimers), while "Teenage Mutant Ninja Turtles III" and a Listerine TV commercial popularized "Tarzan Boy" (Baltimora).

It was also the year Salt-N-Pepa teamed with En Vogue on "Whatta Man"; "Jessie" (Joshua Kadison) explained the satisfaction of a woman to complicate your life; "Two Princes" (The Spin Doctors); "What's Up?" (4 Non Blondes); "Cannonball" (The Breeders;) and "If I Had No Loot" (Tony Toni Tone).

After 22 years at the helm of the syndicated dance series "Soul Train", Don Cornelius relinquished his duties to a weekly guest host.

1994

Just as Nirvana's unplugged performance of "All Apologies" was taking off at MTV, Kurt Cobain's suicide at age 27 on April 5 marked a tragic end to the grunge culture. Troubled for years by unexplained stomach pains, Cobain had resorted to heroin resulting in several near overdoses. Along with the singer's alienation over the public misinterpreting his work, these factors conspired for a life of private torment.

Ironically, the attention focused on his widow, Courtney Love, resulted in the commercial breakthrough for her group Hole ("" Doll House"), as well as The Meat Puppets ("Backwater") who Cobain had praised as his favorite band shortly before his death.

With the central figure of the grunge movement gone, music was left to twist in a dozen directions. Offspring ("Come Out And Play") and Live ("Selling The Drama") incorporated elements of grunge into their style. But emerging acts such as Green Day were pushing in a punk direction with "Basket case", MTV's Top Video for 1994. Acts with a more positive outlook began to emerge including Collective Soul ("Shine"), Des'ree ("You Gotta Be"), Weezer ("Buddy Holly") and Deadeye Dick ("New Age Girl").

Still, pop dominated with the year's best selling single, "I Swear" (All-4-One), the Babyface ballad "I'll Make Love To You" (Boyz II Men) which remained at #1 longer than any other hit that year—14 weeks—and Hootie & The Blowfish's debut album, "Cracked Rear View", which sold an unbelievable 16 million copies!

It was the year of giant dance hits like "100% Pure Love" (Crystal Waters), "Another Night" (Real McCoy), "The Sign" (Ace of Base), the #1 hit on the Billboard Pop Chart for 1994, "Lucas With The Lid Off" (Lucas), and "Get Ready For This" (2 Unlimited) which became rock & roll's third basketball sports anthem.

Riding the dance frenzy, "The Grind" on MTV staged its most elaborate dance number at Spring Break '94. On three separate stages, all of the series best known dancers gave a mass performance which was almost too much for the viewer to take in. Aileen Mateo, Natasha Seigal, Danielle Flora, Melissa Fields, Niko Kearns, Xavi Rodriguez, Leida Villegas and Asia Hernandez were among the cast who starred in that incredible moment.

The year's most profound video "Crazy" (Aerosmith) portrayed two girls (Alicia Silverstone and Steven Tyler's daughter Liv) escaping a repressive school environment to get some kicks. Within a year, Liv Tyler would be one of the hottest names in acting and modeling.

A 90s touchstone was the short-lived TV series "My So Called Life" starring Claire Danes. To many, its 19 episodes were a true reflection of what it was like to be young in the 90s.

TLC's sophomore effort, "Crazy Sexy Cool", was released just weeks after group member Lisa "Left Eye" Lopes torched the mansion of her boyfriend, football wide receiver Andre Rison. The album's first hit, "Creep", inspired a line of pajamas like those worn in the video—creepwear.

It was the year Melissa Ethridge declared she was gay

with the album "Yes I Am"; Coolio sought to escape from redundant gangsta rap trappings with "Fantastic Voyage"; Pearl Jam's "Vitalogy" album was released first on vinyl to attempt to breathe life into that form; Sheryl Crow's memorable debut with the hits "All I Wanna Do" and "Strong Enough"; and the Babyface ballad "Take A Bow" (Madonna).

Even the skeptics had to admit that 1994 was a banner year for independent music, acts existing just below the radar with their own fan base. Some of the best tracks included "Message Man" (The Subdudes), "Even Now" (Frogpond), "Come True" (Zuzu's Petals), "Righteous Love" (Michael Hill's Blues Mob),"Strange Conversation" (Ted Hawkins), "Cannot Love You Enough" (The Willy Wisely Trio), and "One For Her One For Him" (The Starkweathers).

1995

For the first time, the #1 song on the Billboard Pop Chart and MTV's top Video of the Year were the same hit—"Gangsta's Paradise" (Coolio), a repudiation of gangsta rap and the violent street culture. Another first took place in July when "You Are Not Alone" (Michael Jackson) became the first song in the history of the Billboard Pop Chart to debut at #1.

1995 was the year the Latino community mourned the death of Tejano singing star Selena who was murdered by a business associate on March 31, just weeks before her first songs in English, "I Could Fall In Love" and "Dreaming Of You", introduced her to a larger audience.

A loving tribute, the 1997 movie "Selena starring Jennifer Lopez, portrayed her death as a performance interrupted at mid-song.

The year's top female artist, Alanis Morrissette, achieved phenomenal success with the album "Jagged Little Pill" and it angry debut hit "You Oughta Know" based on a diary she kept after a breakup. Her subsequent hits included "Hand In My Pocket" with its kindred oxymorons and "Ironic" regarding everyday inconsistencies.

1995 would be remembered for the NBC TV midseason replacement "Friends" and its widely successful theme "I'll Be There For You" (The Rembrandts); teen girl singers Brandy ("Baby") and Monica ("Don't Take It Personal") and the BET series "Caribbean Rhythms" with Rachel Stuart which helped to launch the hits "Shy Guy" (Diana King) and "Pull Up To The Bumper" (Patra).

The movie "Panther" included the hit "Freedom", the most moving ensemble recording of the decade featuring En Vogue, Salt-N-Pepa, TLC, Zhane, Jade, Vanessa Williams and many others.

Statements that framed the year included "Waterfalls" (TLC), an all-purpose warning not the risk your life for a momentary thrill; "Good" (Better Than Ezra), putting the most positive light on the breakup of a relationship; and "I Kissed A Girl" (Jill Sobule), revealing the gay inclinations existing beneath the surface of the straight community.

Among the more memorable videos – "Just Like Anyone" (Soul Asylum) in which a woman transformed a handicap, wings, into an advantage, and "It's Oh So Quiet"

(Bjork) featuring an offbeat dance number in a tire store while the crescendo and tempo of the music fluctuated to illustrate the ups and downs of 90s romance.

It was the year of the Liv Tyler movie, "Empire Records", featuring the hits "Til I Hear It From You" (The Gin Blossoms) and "A Girl Like You" (Edwyn Collins); the year that former Nirvana drummer Dave Grohl returned with The Foo Fighters ("I'll Be Around"); a big year for Babyface penning the hits "Water Runs Dry" (Boyz II Men), "Someone To Love" (Jon B.) and "Diggin' On You" (TLC).

Other acts that made a major impact included The Presidents Of The United States Of America ("Lump"), Elastica ("Connection"), Bush ("Glycerine"), The Dave Matthews Band ("What Would You Say"), The Goo Goo Dolls ("Name"), Collective Soul ("December"), Del Amitri ("Roll To Me") and Blessed Union Of Souls ("Let Me Be The One").

In Cleveland during the Labor Day weekend, The Rock and Roll Hall of Fame opened with an all-star concert featuring Bruce Springsteen, Chuck Berry and Eric Burdon. Meanwhile, the Internet flashed the decade's best story of coincidence—that the songs from the 1973 album "Dark Side Of The Moon" (Pink Floyd) serve as an unintentional soundtrack to the 1939 movie, "The Wizard Of Oz" when the album is played in synchronicity with the film. More than a half dozen parallels were discovered between the song lyrics and the action in the film.

It was the year the syndicated radio series, "American Top 40", ended its 25-year run, although Casey

Kasem would reactivate the name in 1998 for his countdown show. But it was local radio in 1995 that would exert the most impact on the following year.

Chip Erickson, an ad salesman for KUBE FM, Seattle returned from his vacation with a song that was all the rage in Mexico—"Macarena" (Los Del Rio). The station staged a Macarena night at a local restaurant and soon the song was the most requested at KUBE.

With the video airing on the Spanish language TV network Univision and the song spreading nationwide as an underground dance club hit, a funky Americanized version "the bayside boys mix" was put together by two Miami disc jockeys and that version cracked the Billboard Hot 100 in September where it remained for 20 weeks, peaking at #45, as close as a song gets to being a hit while still remaining unknown to the general public. But it wouldn't be a secret much longer.

1996

For a trend that had swept through Spanish speaking countries like no other, the Macarena had just missed cracking the Top Forty and by late January had tumbled from the Chart, seemingly over with before it had started. Few Anglos had heard it, and the Hispanic population had moved on. Although the dance clubs never gave up on it, the Macarena appeared to have missed its moment.

Then major league baseball, looking for an audience participation event to fire up the crowd prior to the game, began blasting "Macarena (Bayside Boys Mix)" (Los Del

Rio) through its public address systems and the crowd enthusiastically danced along. Media attention of the phenomenon brought the song back to the Billboard Pop Chart where it became the year's best selling single (4 million copies) and the Top Hit on the Billboard Pop Chart for 1996.

That year the Macarena turned up in every facet of American life—the Olympics, Green Bay Packer games, the MDA telethon, the Democratic National Convention, Brandy's UPN sitcom "Moesha", and Hawaiian Punch commercials. There were also rap, country and Christmas variations of the song. Unlike the Twist which was a half dozen separate songs, the Macarena was one song in a half dozen versions. But the year was more than just two middle-aged Spaniards redefining the perimeters of cool.

Three albums scored a major impact. "Tragic Kingdom" (No Doubt) chronicled the breakup of vocalist Gwen Stefani and bass player Tony Kanal in the highly personalized hits "Just A Girl", "Spiderwebs" and "Don't Speak". Briefly ska bands fed off the sound.

With the album "Sublime", the little known cult band achieved the perfect balance of hard rock, rap and reggae on the hits "What I Got", "Santeria" and "Wrong Way".

It was also the year of the giant Oasis album "What's The Story, Morning Glory?" featuring a vocal style patterned after The Beatles on hits like "Wonderwall", "Champagne Supernova" and "Don't Look Back In Anger".

In spite of all the great music, problems were

abounding. On September 7 in Las Vegas, rapper Tupac Shakur, 25, was gunned down a little less than a month after completing the video "I Ain't Mad At Cha" which predicted his death by the gun. The bankruptcies of Hammer, TLC and Toni Braxton shined the spotlight on questionable contracts signed by artists making them responsible for the expenses incurred with record promotion, touring and making of music videos, reducing their profits.

1996 was the year Wal-Mart refused to sell the album "Sheryl Crow" because of the song "Love Is A Good Thing" alluding to children killing each other with a gun purchased from the discount chain. The Fugees and White Zombie were among acts that either cleaned up their lyrics or album covers to appease Wal-Mart.

Among the memorable videos – "Ironic" (Alanis Morrissette), MTV's Top Video for 1996; "Big Me" (The Foo Fighters) satirizing those over-enthusiastic Mentos candy commercials; and "Aeroplane" (The Red Hot Chili Peppers), a tribute to the aquatic musicals of Esther Williams.

At the movies, the Tom Hanks film "The Thing You Do!" charted the rise and fall of a fictitious one-hit group during 1964. Adam Schlesinger wrote the film's theme while enjoying dual success with his own group, Fountains Of Wayne ("Leave The Biker").

The gospel-influenced "I Believe I Can Fly" (R. Kelly) made its way from an animated Bugs Bunny film "SpaceJam" to black church services. Other highlights from 1996 included "No Diggety" (Blackstreet) with its blend of blues, rap and gospel; the decades' hottest blues hit "Give Me One Reason" (Tracy Chapman); Michael Jackson's nephews making peerless harmony as 3T ("Anything"); Bob Dylan's son Jakob fronting The Wallflowers ("One Headlight"); the 80s cult group The BoDeens with "Closer To Free"; the theme from the TV series "Party Of Five"; "Lovefool" (The Cardigans) from the film "Romeo + Juliet"; "I Love You Always Forever" (Donna Lewis); and a hit dedicated to all of the stupid people in the world, "Banditos" (The Refreshments).

1997

The unexpected death of Diana Spencer, the Princess of Wales, in an automobile accident plunged the world into mourning. At her memorial service, Elton John performed a revised version of "Candle In The Wind", a song originally written about Marilyn Monroe. The new version of "Candle In The Wind" backed with "Something About The Way You Look Tonight" (Elton John) became the fastest selling single in history with sales of 3.4 million during its first week of release in the U.S.; the biggest selling single of all time (40 million copies); and the top hit on the Billboard Pop Chart for 1997. It raised $100 million for a charitable foundation established by the late princess.

Grief was also the underpinning for MTV's top video for 1997 "I'll Be Missing You" (Puff Daddy and Faith Evans featuring 112), a tribute to 24-year-old Christopher Wallace (The Notorious B.I.G.) who was gunned down March 9 on a Los Angeles street. Rumors abounded about a connection between this murder and the death of Tupac Shakur the year before, but no arrest was made in either case. Puff Daddy was responsible for mainstreaming rap while at the same time deriding the process in "It's All About The Benjamins".

With the album "Backstreet Boys", the boy band sound arrived. "Quit Playing Games With My Heart", "As Long As You Love Me" and "I'll Never Break Your Heart" were the hits that sprung from this first effort. Lou Pearlman developed both The Backstreet Boys and "N'Sync, schooling the inexperienced teenagers in the ways of show business. After both groups achieved success, they severed all ties with Pearlman whose contracts took a large amount of their salaries and profits from merchandising.

The feel good story of 1997 was from folksinger Jewel Kilcher. In the year that it took for her 1995 album "Pieces Of You" to break through, Jewel went from living on the beach in a Volkswagen van with her mother to having the 1997 hit "You Were Meant For Me" backed with "Foolish Games" to playing to an audience of 300,000 at The Blockbuster Music "Rock Fest" in Fort Worth, Texas on the same bill with The Wallflowers, No Doubt, Collective Soul and Bush.

Meanwhile, Sarah McLachlan ("Building A Mystery") founded Lilith Fair, a concert tour focusing exclusively on female artists. Jewel was also in the lineup, as well as Paula Cole ("Where Have All The Cowboys Gone?"), Meredith Brooks ("Bitch") and Fiona Apple ("Criminal"), the song with the year's best opening line; "I've been a bad, bad girl…"

Teen pop acts for the year included The Spice Girls

("Say You'll Be There"), Hanson ("mmm…Bop") and Swedish teen-throb Robyn ("Do You Know What It Takes").

More adventurous efforts included the rap/rock hit "Fly" (Sugar Ray); the cool jazz of "Virtual Insanity" (Jamiroquai); a hit about the lost idealism of the 70s, "Walkin' On The Sun" (Smash Mouth); India's most profound musical moment "Brimful Of Asha" (Cornershop); the teen abortion ballad "Brick" (Ben Folds Five); "Volcano Girls" (Veruca Salt); a look back at 60s Pop, "How Bizarre" (OMC) and the 1950s Latin sound with "Hell" (The Squirrel Nut Zippers).

It was the year Janet Jackson brought back the dance beat with "Together Again"; "Tubthumping" (Chumbawumba) and "Semi Charmed Life" (Third Eye Blind) made statements of positive resolve; "Stomp" (God's Property) became the first gospel video to make the MTV rotation; "Silver Springs" (Fleetwood Mac), a 20-year-old track omitted from the "Rumours" LP became a hit; and "I Don't Need To Know" (Lady Saw), one of the last new acts broken by "Caribbean Rhythms" before its cancellation by BET.

VH-1 and Gay Rosenthal Productions premiered "Behind The Music", a weekly version of the classic rock scenario—too much too early in life, the downward spiral of sex and substance abuse and, whenever possible, the comeback (usually in a stage production of "Joseph And The Amazing Technicolor Dreamcoat"). The show put acts like Def Leppard back on the Chart again while earning the highest ratings for any program on the network.

1998

"Thank U." (Alanis Morissette) redefined the word 'hit'. Following the success of the songs "Don't Speak" (No Doubt), "Lovefool" (The Cardigans) and "Time Of Your Life" (Green Day) – songs that had never been released as singles yet were all the rage of radio and MTV – "Thank U." caused Billboard Magazine to include for the first time popular album tracks that receive massive airplay and spur sales. Reflecting this change in philosophy, "The Hot 100 Singles Chart" was rechristened "The Hot 100" in December. At this same time, Lee Ann Rimes' 1997 hit "How Do I Live", written by Diane Warren, concluded 69 weeks on the Chart, a new all-time record, proving the single was far from dead.

When 1998 began, Britney Spears was a little-known singer performing shopping mall concerts to promote her upcoming debut album. All of this changed with the video "Baby One More Time" where she danced the high school halls in a tie-up blouse, performed acrobatics and moaned in a more worldly voice than most 17-year-olds. Within weeks, the song was #1 and Britney was on a sultry Rolling Stone cover. One of her later hits, "I'm Not A Girl, Not Yet A Woman", explained the balancing act she tried to achieve. After 1999, the high school girl in the tie-up blouse had vanished, replaced by the "Toxic" femme fatale.

Boy band mania grew in 1998 with N Sync ("Tearin' Up My Heart"), 98 Degrees ("Because Of You") and Five ("When The Lights Go Out"). A rock & roll mainstay—the cover record—resulted in "Torn", one of the year's biggest hits. The British band Ednaswap who had written and originated the song failed to mine commercial success in four separate singles versions. When a former Australian soap opera actress Natalie Imbruglia swept Europe with her cover version, it proved to be a quick leap to MTV and pop success.

An overwhelming feeling sweeping music in 1998 was that we'd heard it all before. Embedded with "Never Ever" (All Saints) was the time honored hymn "Amazing Grace". Spacehog flirted with the ghost of Queen in "Mungo City". "The Way" (Fastball) served as a kind of "Besame Mucho" for its day, while your grandfather's jitterbug records from the 1940s seemed the underpinning for hits like "Jump Jive N' Wail" (The Brian Setzer Orchestra) and "Zoot Suit Riot" (Cherry Poppin' Daddies).

The overworked term "alternative" was defined by acts like Matchbox 20 ("3 a.m."), Everclear ("I Will Buy You A New Life"), The Tuesdays ("It's Up To You") and in a lighter vein, Barenaked Ladies ("One Week"). Proving that rock eats its own, The New Radicals appeared out of nowhere with the hit "You Get What You Give", putting down everyone from Hanson to Marilyn Manson.

Other highlights included the top hit on the Billboard Pop Chart for 1998, "Too Close" (Next); MTV's Top Video for the year, "The Boy Is Mine" (Brandy and Monica); Hole's first album in four years, "Celebrity Skin"; Semisonic's ode to the last bar call, "Closing Time"; Madonna (of all people) telling us to slow down in the video "Ray Of Light"; a stripper balancing the demands of career and family in the video "Turn The Page" (Metallica); "Every Morning" (Sugar Ray) paying homage to Malo's 1972 hit "Suavacito".

For many the action was shifting to the Internet. By 1998, Web Radio was delving more deeply into music than any conventional outlet. Seated at the computer, millions explored the hip hop underground of "Rap Week"; heavy metal KNAC, world music from The Netherland's DFM or Radio Free Kansas, music from India on Navrang Radio and dance beats ranging from jungle to acid house on the British site Interface.

1999

His performance of "The Cup Of Life" at the Grammy Awards not only introduced Ricky Martin to a wider Anglo audience, it also opened the door to a year when Hispanic artists ruled the Pop Chart including Jennifer Lopez ("Waiting For Tonight"), Enrique Iglesias ("Bailamo"), Marc Anthony ("I Need To Know"), the return of Carlos Santana in a duet with Matchbox 20's Rob Thomas ("Smooth") and "Livin' La Vida Loca" (Ricky Martin).

Lou Bega wasn't Hispanic, but he fed off the same wave by adding lyrics to a little known Perez Prado instrumental from 1949, "Mambo No. 5 (a little bit of...)".

The most unique strategy for success belonged to Christina Aguilera. Messages posted on various Internet web sites urged the public to saturate radio stations with requests for her debut hit "Genie In A Bottle". At the same time, her record company arranged a series of concerts specifically for members of the music press to generate buzz about the teenager's remarkable vocal ability. "Genie In A Bottle" vaulted to #1 as the pop culture braced for the inevitable Britney/Christina feud.

The disagreement was between the fans, not the performers. The same fervor applied to the boy bands like 98 Degrees ("The Hardest Thing"), LFO ("Summer Girls") and The Backstreet Boys with MTV's Top Video for 1999, "I Want It That Way".

Beneath the pop calm, a hot issue was brewing on the Internet. Complete albums such as "hours…" (David Bowie) and "There's A Poison Going On" (Public Enemy) resulted in 17 million music files being downloaded daily. Free downloads caused the most stir.

150,000 free downloads of "Free Girl Now" (Tom Petty) during its first three days on MP3.com propelled the album to a #10 debut, yet Warner Brothers forced Petty off the Internet viewing the giveaway as a violation of contract.

Radio stations aired unreleased tracks by Metallica and rapper Eminem downloaded free from Napster Inc., drawing separate lawsuits for copyright infringement from both the RIAA (Recording Industry Association of America) and Metallica. Napster argued that it only provided the site, not the content. The question for the courts to decide—was it theft or a new way of doing business where artists would derive their profits from corporate sponsorships rather than the sale of CDs.

Metallica, The Goo Goo Dolls, Offspring and Aerosmith battled their record companies over control of their web sites with millions of dollars in music, merchandise and promotion hanging in the balance. Recording acts viewed the Internet as a direct link to the public while record companies worried it could render the

CD obsolete.

Defining the direction of music during 1999 was even more daunting. 49-year-old Cher scored the #1 hit on the Billboard Pop Chart for 1999 with "Believe". Smash Mouth ("All Star") and Sugar Ray ("Someday") confounded the critics who had earlier written them off as one-hit wonders. Sixpence None The Richer switched from contemporary Christian music to pop for the romantic ballad "Kiss Me" while Mulberry Lane defied their record company's original plan to mold them into a country group by releasing the pop hit "Harmless".

TLC gave freeloading boyfriends the once over with "Scrubs" and depicted the negative aspects of the pursuit of glamour in "Unpretty". Video landmarks included "All The Small Things" (Blink 182) for its satire of boy bands; "Learn To Fly" (The Foo Fighters) where Dave Grohl plays most of the characters, male and female; and "So Pure" (Alanis Morissette) paying homage to thirty years of dance evolution.

Also during 1999, Guns N' Roses released their first new song in five years, "Oh My God"; Jewel had a bestselling poetry book, "A Night Without Armor" and Fiona Apple made history with the world's longest album title: "When the pawn hits the conflict he thinks like a king what he knows throws the blows when he goes to the fight and he'll win the whole thing 'fore he enters the ring there's nobody to batter when your mind is your might so when you go solo you hold your own hand and remember that depth is the greatest of heights and if you know where you stand then you know where to land and if you fail it won't matter 'cuz you'll know that you're right."

2000

Does the world owe you free music? According to separate court rulings in 2000 against MP3.com and the following year against Napster, the answer is 'no'. The two top Internet services involved in free download were ordered to remove copyrighted music from their files. Although other smaller services were waiting in the wings, the future didn't look bright for free downloads.

If the downloads had any impact on record sales, it didn't show. Setting a new record for first week sales, the album "No Strings Attached" (N Sync) sold 2.4 million records. "Black And Blue" (The Backstreet Boys), "Oops I Did It Again" (Britney Spears) and "The Slim Shady LP" (Eminem) also sold a million or more during the first week of release.

Eminen dominated the moment with songs about murdering his wife and raping his mother. Christina Aguilera and gays were among the targets of his vitriol. Even overly obsessed fans got a working over in his video "Stan".

At the other musical extreme, "Who Let The Dogs Out" (The Baha Men) took the call and response of Trinidad carnival and refocused it in every phase of American life from its use in sports stadium pregame festivities to its inclusion in the children's movie "Rugrats In Paris". The song allowed women to give men a little good natured ribbing.

Like The Baha Men, fellow Caribbean performer Shaggy also peaked after nearly a decade with the singles "Dance And Shout" and "It Wasn't Me", while long-time country diva Shelby Lynne went pop with "Gotta Get Back".

It was a year with something for everyone. Alt-rock with No Doubt ("Bathwater"), Matchbox Twenty ("If You're Gone") and Ultimate Fakebook ("Tell Me What You Want"). More pop oriented material with Vitamin C ("Graduation – Friends Forever") and Faith Hill with the #1 hit on the Billboard Pop Chart for 2000, "Breathe".

It had to happen sooner or later. On the week of July 29, the Top Album on the Billboard Hot 200 was "Now That's What I Call Music 4", a compilation album featuring previously released singles by Britney Spears, Blink 182, Marc Anthony and Eiffel 65. It was the first time that a compilation album of previously released material topped the Chart.

Even though MTV was becoming more about lifestyle programming and less about music, its boy band parody 2gether featuring pudgy, balding comedian Kevin Farley registered impressive sales of the album "2gethr Again" featuring cuts like "The Hardest Part Of Breaking Up (Is Getting Back Your Stuff)", Anastacia, a runner-up in MTV's 1999 talent contest show "The Cut", also made ripples in 2000 with her dance single "I'm Outta Love".

In Seattle, a $240 million museum, *The Experience Music Project,* opened with a concert featuring Alanis Morissette, James Brown, Bo Diddley, The Kingsmen, The Eurythmics and Paul Revere & The Raiders. Conceived by Microsoft founder Paul Allen, the museum features 80,000 artifacts including Elvis' black leather jacket, Janis Joplin's floral bell bottoms and the Fender Stratocaster that Jimi

Hendrix played at Woodstock.

Technology issues in the year 2000 included the SMDI Phase 1, a watermark embedded in CDs to prevent piracy; DVD audio titles simulating the surround sound effect of movie theaters and a higher grade of bootleg recordings thanks to the ALD device at concerts provided for the hearing impaired.

The year 2000 also marked the end of an international manhunt that had gone on for a year when Mexican singer Gloria Trevi and her manager Sergio Andrade were arrested in Brazil. Andrade was wanted for the rape of a 13-year-old girl. Trevi's name had been used in the phony talent school that Andrade had used to attract women. Trevi would be released from prison in 2004 for lack of evidence.

2001

"Hanging By A Moment" (Lifehouse) proved to be more than just the top song on the Billboard Pop Chart for 2001. The hit took on an eerier connotation in the aftermath of the September 11 terrorist attacks that killed nearly 3,000 in New York City and Washington, D.C., a day when the whole country was hanging by a moment. For that reason, the song was temporarily removed from the playlists at many radio stations.

September 11 jarred the country in many ways. "America: A Tribute To Heroes" (September 21) simulcast by more than 25 cable and commercial TV networks raised $140 million for victims of the attack. Paul Simon, Bruce

Springsteen, Stevie Wonder, Tom Petty, John Mellencamp and Billy Joel were among the performers at the solemn event. Taking place only ten days after the tragedy, the concert came off like a funeral with performers and viewers still in a state of shock.

What a difference a month made. VH1's "Concert For New York City" (October 20) dramatized the rebound of the American spirit. Not only did it serve as a triumphant celebration for the city, it sent a message to the terrorists that the buildings collapsed but the country didn't. The latter concert featured comedy skits, short films about New York City and a stellar lineup including Paul McCartney, Mick Jagger and Keith Richards, The Backstreet Boys, Destiny's Child, Eric Clapton, Bon Jovi, Elton John, Janet Jackson, The Goo Goo Dolls and Melissa Etheridge.

Music helped to heal the country. The ensemble recordings "What's Going On – All Star Tribute" organized by Bono and P. Diddy (formerly Puff Daddy) and "What More Can I Give" orchestrated by Michael Jackson benefitted charities helping the victims' families. The Eagles reunited briefly for the single "Hole In The World" which dramatized the moment. And MTV set aside its lifestyle programming briefly for wall-to-wall music videos, realizing the impact of music in those troubled days.

September 11 wasn't the only shocking event of the year. On August 25, 22-year-old pop star Aaliyah perished in a plane crash in the Bahamas. Reports indicated that the plane was carrying too much luggage and too many passengers. Her death came only one month after the release of her latest album and just as she was receiving rave reviews for her acting debut in the movie "Romeo Must Die".

The year's big music trend "neo-soul" signaled a return to the heartfelt R&B of the 60s and 70s, best exemplified by Alicia Keys ("Fallin'") and Blu Cantrell ("Hit 'Em Up Style – Oops"), the latter creating a social stir with its video in which Blu gets revenge on a cheating boyfriend by unloading his possessions at a yard sale and maxing out his Nieman Marcus card.

It was a year of musical surprises. An obscure two-year-old album cut, "Start The Commotion" (The Wise Guys), banking off the "Louie Louie" rhythm reached the Singles Chart after blanketing the airwaves in a Mitsubishi car commercial. Gorillaz, a group represented only by its cartoon namesakes 2D, Murdoc, Russel and Noodle, broke big with the animated video "Clint Eastwood".

Nikka Costa, daughter of Frank Sinatra producer Don Costa, gave men everything they could hope for in the video "Like A Feather", while the Madonna video "What It Feels Like For A Girl" aired only once on MTV and VH1 due to its excessive violence. Michael Jackson made a less than dramatic comeback attempt with "You Rock My World".

2002

The year's biggest star, the Apple iPod and its various clones, was the recording industry's latest attempt to promote legal downloading. Twenty million downloads at $1 a song on Apple's iTunes was fed into the iPod discs that could accommodate 5,000 titles. The consumer could now carry his whole record collection on a single disc in his pocket.

The year's best selling single, "A Moment Like This" (Kelly Clarkson), featured the 20-year-old former cocktail waitress who beat out 10,000 contestants on the Fox summer series *American Idol*. Clarkson was part of a wave of female singers who toned down their sexuality to emphasize their musical artistry including Avril Lavigne ("Complicated"), Michelle Branch ("All You Wanted"), Vanessa Carlton ("A Thousand Miles") and jazz crossover Norah Jones ("Don't Know Why").

Sex didn't disappear. Christina Aguilera showed more skin than ever before in the video "Dirty" but barely made a blip on the radar while 40-year-old Sheryl Crow never looked better than in "Soak Up The Sun", VH1's top video of the year, and "Steve McQueen".

Ashanti ("Foolish") debuted with three singles in the Billboard Top Ten, a feat not witnessed since The Beatles. But when "Soul Train" awarded her The Aretha Franklin Performer Of The Year Award, 19,799 people signed an on-line petition asking for a better candidate.

Statement that framed the year included "No Such Thing" (John Mayer) about the "quarter life crisis", discovering at 25 that life is not the way it is portrayed in high school";

"Days Go By" (Dirty Vegas), a retro 90s dance groove that echoed everywhere from dance clubs to Mitsubishi car commercials; "The Middle" (Jimmy Eat World) serving punk on a melodic hook; and "Work It" (Missy Elliott), an other-worldly rap experience.

During April, for the first time since 1963, no British acts appeared on the Billboard Hot 100 Singles' Chart (the Brits would return in May). MTV announced a tighter playlist -
"The Big 10", videos that would be played more than thirty times a week. Other videos would receive only ten plays a week. The network now expected a record label to make its own promotional push instead of relying on MTV to put an artist over the top.

The death of Lisa "Left Eye" Lopes, 30, in a single car accident on April 25 in La Ceiba, Honduras brought an end to TLC. T-Boz and Chilli completed the album "TLC3D", dedicating their video "Girl Talk" to Lisa.

A 3% decline in record sales during 2001 could be juxtaposed against the emergence of more internet file swapping services like Kazaa, Morpheus and Limewire offering a wider variety of music and videos than legitimate pay services. Twenty percent of the free downloads according to RIAA estimates were from college campuses causing gridlock at many universities. While colleges sought to discourage the practice, advances in digital technology were making it more possible to block free media consumption from both the Internet and cable.

In the meantime, record labels turned to longstanding names to offset the losses. "The Rising" (Bruce Springsteen & The E Street Band) explored the emotions of September 11 giving the Boss his most successful album in years. A remix of little known track "A Little Less Conversation" (Elvis Presley) reached #1 in

England spawning the album "Elvis' 30 #1 Hits" which debuted at #1 in the U.S.

The previously unreleased single "You Know You're Right" (Nirvana) made its way from the Internet to radio to disc while record companies dredged the vaults to produce new compilations by Queen, Fleetwood Mac, The Rolling Stones and Aerosmith.

Other highlights included the #1 hit on the Billboard Pop Chart for 2002, "How You Remind Me" (Nickleback); MTV's top video for the year, "Without Me" (Eminem); the music video "Hands Clean" (Alanis Morissette) tracing the evolution of a song from its creation through its manufacture, marketing and promotion; and the "Be You" Dr. Pepper commercial sung by Sugar Ray's Mark McGrath paying homage to Buddy Holly and rock & roll.

2003

What seemed like a bad idea to some turned into a good career move for Hilary Duff. After the box office success of "The Lizzie McGuire Movie", the 15-year-old actress announced that she was leaving the Disney Channel series to pursue a movie and recording career. By year's end she was everywhere—the fifth best selling single of the year, "So Yesterday", its #1 album "Metamorphosis", her own one-hour special on the WB network and a supporting role in the Steve Martin movie "Cheaper By The Dozen."

The country group The Dixie Chicks made a pop breakthrough with a cover of Fleetwood Mac's "Landslide" at the same time that the group's lead singer, Natalie Mains, expressed her views against the war in Iraq by telling an audience in England that she was ashamed President Bush was from their home state of Texas. Practically overnight country radio banned The Chicks while the pop audience pushed their records higher up the Chart.

On February 20, 100 people died and 200 were injured when highly flammable soundproofing material was ignited by a pyrotechnics display during a concert by Great White ("Once Bitten") at a concert club named The Station in West Warwicke, Rhode Island. The group's manager received a ten-year prison sentence.

Rapper 50 Cent ruled with "In Da Club", the #1 hit on the Billboard Pop Chart for 2003 and MTV's top video for the year from his album "Get Rich Or Die Tryin'", Billboard's Top Album of the year.

"Hey Ya" (Outkast) had everything "shaking like a Polaroid picture". The video "Stacy's Mom" (Fountains Of Wayne) showed a teenager's futile sexual fantasy for an adult woman. "Clocks" (Coldplay) was the year's most inescapable song, released twice—first in studio form then as a live performance.

For the very first time, on the week of October 11 all of the positions in Billboard's Top Ten were occupied by black artists, including Nelly and Beyonce. The two top selling singles of the year, "This Is The Night/Bridge Over Troubled Water" (Clay Aiken) and "Flying Without Wings/Superstar" (Ruben Studdard) were both by *American Idol* finalists. But both would have to go a long way to catch up with the original "Idol", Kelly Clarkson, who added to her string of hits in 2003 with "Miss

Independent".

The year's most overhyped moment took place at the MTV Video Music Awards when Madonna concluded her performance by kissing Britney Spears on the lips while Spears' former boyfriend, Justin Timberlake, looked on in disgust from the audience. Britney and Madonna teamed again for Britney's video "Me Against The Music".

It was the year of Lisa Marie Presley, Elvis' daughter, with "Lights Out"; "When I'm Gone" (3 Doors Down) filmed aboard the aircraft carrier The U.S.S. Washington to show support for the military; "Dance With My Father" (Luther Vandross), an intensely personal song about the father who left him at age 7, recorded shortly before Vandross' debilitating stroke; Pink as the bawdy wild west saloon girl spoiling for a fight in the video "Trouble"; and a VH1 documentary about Warren Zevon's final album recorded as the singer was slowly wasting away from cancer.

The Recording Industry Association of America took the most excessive illegal downloaders to court in 2003. Among them were college students, a pre-teen living in a housing project, and a grandfather who had no idea what his grandchildren were doing at his computer. The lawsuits were working, resulting in 4 million fewer illegal downloads in 2003. Even Napster returned as a pay service charging 99 cents for a song or $9.99 for an album.

Other highlights included "The Hardest Button to Button" (The While Stripes), "Are You Gonna Be My Girl" (Jet), "Blueside" (Rooney) and "Special" (Wilshire).

Forty years after their initial splash, The Beatles and

The Rolling Stones were still sending ripples through the industry. In England and The Netherlands, a cache of over 500 unreleased Beatle tapes missing since 1969 surfaced in a raid on music pirates while in the U.S., The Rolling Stones concert album and DVD released exclusively at Best Buy prompted several major competitors to remove all Stones records from their shelves in protest.

2004

It would always be remembered as the Super Bowl where no one remembers the game, only the controversial halftime show where Justin Timberlake tore away the upper portion of Janet Jackson's dress exposing her right breast to an audience of millions. CBS, the network carrying the Super Bowl, received a $550,000 fine from the FCC which was rescinded by a judge in 2008. Several other fines were levied, some for broadcasts several years old.

MTV temporarily moved its more salacious videos to late evening, while the music video "This Love" (Maroon 5) addressed the uncertain social climate by releasing two versions, one with a camera trick covering up partial nudity. It was the "wardrobe malfunction" heard 'round the world.

The rest of the year belonged to Usher with the top two songs on the Billboard Hot 100 for 2004—1) "Yeah" and 2) "Burn". Together the songs spent 20 consecutive weeks at #1, the longest run for any act in the history of the chart. Two other Usher hits "Confessions Part II" and "My Boo" spent an additional 7 weeks at #1 while the album that housed them all, "Confessions", became

Billboard's Top Album for 2004.

During an October appearance on NBC's "Saturday Night", Ashlee Simpson ("Pieces Of Me") walked off the stage after the wrong track was played. Viewers could hear Ashlee's voice while she was making no effort to sing, reminding many of the Milli Vanilli debacle.

The year's most riveting music video, "World On Fire" (Sarah McLachlan), donated its $150,000 budget to charitable causes in Africa, spending only $15 on the video itself. "The Reason" (Hoobastank) served as a primer on how to transform a fake automobile accident into a jewel heist, while "1985" (Bowling For Soup) staged a good-natured satire of the 1980s music scene with the year's most profound lyric, "When did Motley Crue become classic rock?"

It wasn't a good year for Britney Spears. Britney married childhood friend Jason Alexander in January, only to have the marriage annulled 55 hours later. After breaking a leg during the filming of a music video, Britney cancelled the remainder of her summer concert tour. On September 18, she walked down the aisle a second time with Kevin Federline, a backup dancer for Justin Timberlake, Britney's ex-boyfriend. The marriage ended in divorce two years later.

Fueled by the iPod craze, legal downloads were outpacing CD singles in sales.

2005

Benefit concerts for the hurricane ravaged south and international tsunami relief sparked a philanthropy movement during 2005. One concert, "Live 8" on July 2, a project of The Band-Aid Trust, took a totally different direction. Instead of asking for donations to aid the African continent, viewers were asked to contact the heads of eight industrial nations meeting at that week's G-8 Conference to make available more money for African humanitarian relief. Twenty-five billion dollars was requested by concert organizers. The G-8 Conference answered with $50 billion.

Mariah Carey made an incredible rebound to the top after several uneven years with "We Belong Together", the #1 hit on The Billboard Pop Chart for 2005 and VH1's top video of the year. "Since U Been Gone" (Kelly Clarkson) was the year's most frequently aired hit due in part to the memorable music video where a vengeful Kelly trashes the apartment of a cheating boyfriend who threw her over.

Enduring images for the year included "Wake Me Up When September Ends" (Green Day) with its riveting portrayal of a personal relationship weathering a young man's military service in Iraq; "Hollaback Girl" (Gwen Stefani), a raucous tribute to cheerleaders, drum majorettes and the spelling of the word "bananas"; and "Doncha" (The Pussycat Dolls) with its lyric "Doncha wish your girlfriend was hot like me?", a universal turnoff to women listeners.

The soundtrack album "Garden State" featuring The

Shins, Remy Zero and Frou Frou sold more than a million copies. The album began as a mix tape of songs by Zach Braff to sell movie studios on the concept of the film by the same name which became an important generational love story.

The album "From The Ground Up" (Antigone Rising) became the first record marketed exclusively through The Starbucks Coffee chain. The conglomerate enjoyed previous success marketing albums that were already in general release.

"Trapped In The Closet" (R. Kelly) was a multi-part music video with a simple plot—everyone in the video was cheating on everyone else. Seven chapters of the video were televised by year's end with further installments promised.

Both TLC and INXS chose new group members during their respective summer TV reality series; the music video "Streets Of Love" (The Rolling Stones) premiered on an October episode of the NBC TV daytime drama, "Days Of Our Lives"; and Dick Clark returned to anchor "New Year's Rockin' Eve" on ABC TV after his absence in 2004 due to a stroke.

2006

"Not Ready To Make Nice" (The Dixie Chicks) and their anti George Bush documentary "Shut Up And Sing!" stoked the controversy anew in 2006. Any hope to repair the relationship with country radio stations was over. The video received heavy airplay on VH1 and MTV as well as pop radio, causing the album "Taking The Long Way" to reach #16 on Billboard's Year End Chart for 2006. The Dixie Chicks received five Grammy Awards in 2007.

The soundtrack to the Disney Channel movie "High School Musical" sold 6 million copies, placing nine original hits on The Billboard Hot 100, more than any other soundtrack in Chart history. Even before the movie aired, the track "Breaking Free" was given away free on the HSM web site, launching the worldwide craze for the "tween" album.

Newcomer K. T. Tunstall was omnipresent. The ABC TV series "Men In Trees" helped to make a hit of her track "Black Horse And The Cherry Tree" while the network's "Ugly Betty" launched the follow-up "Suddenly I See". "Grey's Anatomy" featured three other Tunstall songs, "Other Side Of The World", "Universe & U" and "Miniature Disasters".

"The Grey's Anatomy Original Soundtrack Volume 1 and 2" made hits of several songs, most notably "How To Save A Life" (The Fray) and "Chasing Cars" (Snow Patrol). Another major musical innovator, Timbaland, brought dance beats to several of the year's biggest hits including "Promiscuous" (Nelly Furtado), "Sexyback" (Justin Timberlake) and "Wait A Minute" (The Pussycat Dolls).

Indelible images for the year included the music video "Here It Goes Again" (OK Go) with choreography on four exercise treadmills; "Hips Don't Lie" (Shakira), the contemporary belly dancer song and video; "Stupid Girls" (Pink) about women who dumb down for fame; "Call Me

When You're Sober" (Evanscence) for all women who are tired of dating alcoholics; and "Lips Of An Angel" (Hinder), which captured the crisis of dating one girl while not being able to get another out of your mind. On a more serious note, "Waiting For The World To Change" (John Mayer) was a barometer for the frustration being felt by the current generation seeking to have a social impact.

The Nickelback album, "All The Right Reasons", was the unexpected success of the year featuring six Top Forty Hits including "Photograph" and "Savin' Me", a string of hits that continued throughout 2007. It was also a year of overpowering female performances including "Ain't No Other Man" (Christina Aguilera), "Be Without You" (Mary J. Blige) and the showstopper "And I'm Telling You I'm Not Going" (Jennifer Hudson) from the movie "Dreamgirls". The song had added poignancy because Hudson had been a runner-up on *American Idol* and although she received much of the public acclaim, the spotlight also returned to Jennifer Holliday who had originated the song when "Dreamgirls" was a 1980s Broadway production.

Other highlights from 2006 included the #1 hit on the Billboard Pop Chart "Bad Day" (Daniel Powter) from *American Idol*; "Do It To It" (Cherish); "You're Beautiful" (James Blunt); "Dirty Little Secret" (The All American Rejects); "Idlewild" (Outkast); "I Write Sins Not Tragedies" (Panic At The Disco); cult comedian Jack Black as the leader of the ersatz rock band Tenacious D. in the movie, "The Pick Of Destiny"; and heiress/actress Paris Hilton and Brooke Hogan, daughter of wrestler Hulk, both launching singing careers.

2007

On the surface, 2007 appeared no different than any other year. "Irreplaceable" (Beyonce) was the top hit on the Billboard Pop Chart for 2007, while the year's best selling album "Daughtery" spawned six Top Forty hits while selling 2.2 million copies.

"Rehab" (Amy Winehouse) showcased the year's trashy tough cookie, while at the other extreme, "Bubbly" (Colby Calliat) offered the girl next door in a song that first originated at MySpace.com.

Redux hung heavy in the air. "Candyman" (Christina Aguilera) was a taste of 1940s big band swing. "Beautiful Girls" (Sean Kingston) drew from the Stand By Me bass solo. The video "Bonafied Lovin'" (Chromeo) rechanneled the look of Dire Strait's 1985 music video "Money For Nothing".

"1 2 3 4" (Feist) no sooner appeared than it made the jump to a television commercial for the iPod Nano, while a group of celebrities and common folk competed for face time in the video "Rockstar" (Niclelback) celebrating the overindulgence of rock bands. Cutting edge producer/performer Timbaland took an unexpected turn as producer of the soft ballad rock group One Republic ("Apologize").

Beneath the surface, another reality was taking shape. The antiwar song made a return with "Dear Mr. President" (Pink), "Coming Home" (John Legend), "Hands Held High" (Linkin Park) and "Girl America" (Mat

Kearney). Teenage pregnancy became a front burner issue with the movie "Juno" and its cross-generational soundtrack featuring Buddy Holly, The Kinks, The Velvet Underground and Mott The Hoople.

If not dead, the music single was at least missing in action. The download had become the new music single. Music videos were used to anoint a radio airplay "hit", but album sales continued to slump with consumers purchasing only the tracks they wanted via the Internet.

Even the older established acts created an uproar by challenging the way the major labels do business. Paul McCartney departed Capitol for the new record label distributed exclusively at Starbucks Coffee. Madonna bolted Warner Brothers for a $120 million deal with Live Nation. The Eagles marketed their first studio album in nearly thirty years, "Long Road To Eden", exclusively through Wal Mart, while Radiohead released its album "In The Rainbows" as a pay-what-you-wish download.

Other highlights included "Won't Go Home Without You" (Maroon 5); "How Far We've Come" (Matchbox Twenty); and two concerts of note—Led Zeppelin reunited for a one-night concert in England during December, still demonstrating the fire of old, while stateside ticket scalpers outpriced the budgets of tweens and their parents for the Hannah Montana tour.

2008

When her record company asked her to write something of a commercial nature, Sara Barellies responded with "Love Song" where she rebukes her employer: "I'm not going to write you a love song 'cause you want one, 'cause you need one". Epic promoted the track into the seventh biggest hit of the year, an ironic moment in corporate vengeance.

The age of the millennial had arrived, children and grandchildren of baby boomers who formed a pivotal voting block in the election of President Barack Obama. To these children of Columbine, 9/11 and Hurricane Katrina, the world of their parents was ancient history.

Their world was one where most of the music originated from five major record labels, two with overseas ownership—Sony and Capitol, and three spun off from Hollywood movie studios—Warner Brothers, Universal/MCA and Hollywood Records (Disney). Atlantic Records (a division of Warner Brothers) announced that for the first time 50% of its profits were derived from downloads and ringtones, showing how the business was transforming in the 21st century.

But there were still plenty of big records. After at least three false starts as a gospel or country performer, Katy Perry went pop with her summer smash, "I Kissed A Girl". Other acts on the edge included the 60s English groove of Duffy ("Mercy") and the snotty Blondie throwback, The Ting Tings ("Shut Up And Let Me Go").

Kid Rock fused the 70s grooves of Warren Zevon's "Werewolves Of London" to Lynard Skynard's "Sweet Home Alabama" for the inescapable hit, "All Summer Long", which garnered airplay at MTV, VH1 and CMT.

YouTube contributed to the success of several acts

including Beyonce, whose "Single Ladies (Put A Ring On It)" featured the singer in a black leotard dancing maniacally while attracting 22 million viewers and spawning parodies from other YouTube videos and *Saturday Night Live.*

Ingrid Michaelson's music leapt from her MySpace website to the soundtrack of ABC TV's "Grey's Anatomy" to an Old Navy TV commercial that literally vaulted her song "The Way I Am" into the Top Forty. Soon Michaelson was part of the Hotel Café Tour featuring prominent folk artists.

The soundtrack to the movie "Body Of War" featuring Bruce Springsteen, Pearl Jam, Rage Against The Machine, Public Enemy, and Neil Young told the story of a 27-year-old Iraqi war veteran, Thomas Young, paralyzed by a sniper's bullet and his life since then as an antiwar activist lobbying Congress to bring the troops home.

Other highlights included the top hit on the Billboard Pop Chart for 2008, "Low" (Flo-Rida featuring T-Pain), "Love Song" (Sara Barellies), "Sorry (Buckcherry), "Teardrops On My Guitar" (Taylor Swift), and putting her personal troubles aside, Britney Spears back on top with "Womanizer".

Coldplay summed the moment up in three words—"Viva La Vida!", a musical triumph about a historical triumph.

2009

" 'This is it' really means this is it."

...Michael Jackson announcing a series of fifty concerts he was to perform in England to retire from music in triumph. Instead, a little more than twelve hours after a rehearsal at The Staples Center in Los Angeles, Jackson died at age 50 on June 25, 2009.

The Los Angeles County Coroner ruled the death a homicide, possibly caused by a variety of drugs in his system including the powerful anesthetic Propoful which Jackson used to induce sleep. A July 7 memorial service at The Staples Center was carried live on the Internet drawing thousands of fans to Los Angeles in an outpouring of love and adulation not witnessed since Jackson's peak popularity in the 1980s and early 90s.

A film about the preparation for the concert tour "This Is It" opened at #1 weeks later, while four Jackson albums appeared in Billboard's Year End Countdown for 2009 – "Michael Jackson's Number Ones" (#4), "Thriller" (#16), "The Essential Michael Jackson" (#22) and "This Is It" (#45). On December 30, the music video "Thriller" (1983) was named to the film registry of The Library Of Congress, the first music video ever to receive this preservation.

Apart from Jackson's death, the spotlight for 2009 belonged to 19-year-old Taylor Swift whose album "Fearless" was the top album of the year. Its hit, "Love Story", received the most airplay for any song in 2009.

Videos including "You Belong To Me" made her the rare country songbird to rule MTV, where her win for the Best Female Music Video at the VMAs caused a verbal dustup with rapper Kanye West who interrupted her acceptance speech to declare Beyonce more worthy of the award. Swift made light of the event while hosting *Saturday Night Live* days before releasing her Christmas album. She was also the Top Country Act for the year and a frequent presence on a variety of magazine covers.

The Internet continued to wield considerable influence. The YouTube replay of Susan Boyles' performance of "I Dreamed A Dream" from the TV series *Britain's Got Talent* launched the singer's debut album at #1! "My Life Would Suck Without You" (Kelly Clarkson) made the historic jump from #97 to #1 thanks to 280,000 digital downloads and a music video where Clarkson and her boyfriend playfully toss each other's possessions out of their apartment window. The album "My World" (Justin Bieber) had all seven of its tacks reach The Billboard Hot 100 due to the power of Internet users in spite of the reality that few were being aired on the radio.

Of the top four hits for 2009, two belonged to The Black Eyed Peas – "Boom Boom Pow" (#1) and "I Gotta Feeling" (#4), while the other two were by dance diva Lady Gaga – "Poker Face" (#2) and "Let's Dance" (#3). "Poker Face", a song about faking passion during sex, was also VH1s Top Video for 2009.

The sudden diversity in music caused a 17% rise in Top Forty radio formats across the U.S. in 2009 with 944 stations programming the format compared to only 879 the year before. In a single hour, Top Forty could span the hip hop of The Black Eyed Peas ("I Gotta Feeling"), dancebeat with Lady Gaga (Papparazzi"), teen pop with Miley Cyrus ("The Climb"), country by Taylor Swift ("White Horse"), rock with Kings of Leon ("Use Somebody"), electro-pop through Owl City ("Fireflies"), reggae from Michael Franti and Spearhead ("Say Hey [I Love You])" and pop with Katy Perry ("Waking Up In Vegas").

Other highlights from 2009 included the creep out music video "Please Don't Leave Me" (Pink) where a woman holds onto the man she loves through a series of violent acts; "Second Chance" (Shinedown), a song and music video about following your dreams no matter what; "My Flow So Tight" (The Smoke Jumpers), a song with the chorus; "Chris Brown should get his ass kicked" after revelations of Brown's domestic violence against singer Rhianna; and "Celebration" (Madonna), a 2-DVD 47 music video compilation of Madonna's 25-year career spanning a full three-and-a-half hours.

Statements for the year included "If I Were A Boy" (Beyonce) regarding society's double standards for gender and the album "War Child" featuring Duffy, Franz Ferdinand, Estelle and The Yeah Yeah Yeahs, a benefit for the charity War Child International to raise money to aid children in the world's war zones.

2010

The record album and the video identified the song as "F**k You" (Cee Lo Green) while VH1 announced it as "F You". With a title sporting the F bomb, it caused a national dialogue on how it would be announced at the

Grammy Awards, let alone to be mentioned in polite conversation. Still, the song vaulted into the Billboard Top Twenty and garnered regular rotation in the playlists of both MTV and VH1.

For the first time since 1946, a female debut act scored the Top Song of the Year on the Billboard Chart — "Tik Tok" (Ke$ha) followed by a string of dance hits including "Blah Blah Blah", "Take It Off", "My First Kiss" and "We R Who We R".

Close behind the new artist was Billboard's New Artist of 2009, Lady Gaga, with "Bad Romance" and "Alejandro". Her music video "Telephone" cast Gaga and Beyonce as ex-convicts on the run after poisoning the customers of a restaurant.

Rolling Stone's special summer issue featuring a thong-clad gun-toting Gaga sold nearly 250,000 copies, over three times the magazine's monthly average, while her cover for *Cosmopolitan* was their best selling issue of the year.

The television series *Glee* placed six albums and eight singles on the Chart, mostly updates of established standards like the Madonna catalog, "Singing In The Rain" and "I've Had The Time Of My Life".

Grace Potter And The Nocturnals ("Paris Ooh La La") were proclaimed the rock band of the year by Rolling Stone; "Holiday (Vampire Weekend) created the year's standout arrangement; the #1 hit "Firework" (Katy Perry) demonstrated her vocal power; and Weezer had the standout song title of 2010, "(If You're Wondering If I Want To) I Want To."

Chris Brown staged a comeback after his domestic violence debacle with Rhianna on "Yeah X 3" and "Deuces". MTV created the album "Hope For Haiti Now" to benefit the victims of the 2010 earthquake. A total of 65 Christmas albums graced the final Billboard Hot 200 for the year including some original material like "Christmas Lights" (Coldplay).

Billboard's Group of the Year, Lady Antebellum, crossed over from the Country Chart with "Need You Now", "American Honey" and "One Kind Of Love." Teen idol Justin Beiber ("Baby") mass marketed his image in everything from cosmetics to toy doll likeness. Miley Cyrus attempted to leave Hannah Montana behind with "The Climb" and "Party In The U.S.A." The memorable video, "Tighten Up" (The Black Keys) found two adult fathers wrestling each other to the ground for the attention of an attractive woman who happened to be the mother of the little girl over whom their sons just had a dustup.

Hits from previous years lingered around long enough to place in Billboard's Year End Countdown including "Sweet Soul Sister" (Train) and "I Gotta Feeling" (The Black Eyed Peas), while several classic albums reappeared in the listings including "Thriller" (Michael Jackson) and "Exile On Main Street" (The Rolling Stones).

Other highlights included "Live Like We're Dying" (Kris Allen); "Rhythm Of Love" (Plain White T's); "This Afternoon" (Nickelback); "The Only Exception" (Paramore); "Just Haven't Met You Yet" (Michael Buble) and the comeback album, "Soldier Of Love" by 80s great, Sade.

2011

With the year's biggest hit on the Billboard Hot 100, "Rolling In The Deep", and the year's Top Album, "21", British singer Adele framed the universal themes of relationships ending bitterly and women dealing with personal imperfections. Subsequent hits including "Someone Like You" and "Set Fire To The Rain" continued to display Adele's honest emotion-charged vocals while her lyrics drew from a true life breakup that further fueled the fire.

Adele's 2011 included walking the streets of Paris, one of the most romantic cities in the world, while acting out her heartbreak video "Someone Like You", fending off her ex-boyfriend who attempted to claim a percentage for putting her through the hell that inspired her music, and successfully recovering from surgery on her damaged vocal chords which left her temporarily unable to speak or sing at year's end. Her prognosis was for a speedy recovery.

As Adele's star rose, the life of another talented singer ended abruptly. Amy Winehouse died unexpectedly at age 27 from the rigors of alcoholism, continuing the curse of 27 that claimed the lives of Kurt Cobain, Jim Morrison, Brian Jones, Jimi Hendrix and Janis Joplin. Her final hits during 2011 were "Body And Soul" (a duet with Tony Bennett) and a remake of the 1963 hit, "Our Day Will Come".

With "Skyscraper", Disney star Demi Lovato revealed her real-life addiction to "cutting" (self-mutilation) while "Born This Way" (Lady Gaga) provided a voice to everyone abandoned outside the social mainstream. "Last Friday Night (T.G.I.F.)" became the fifth hit from Katy Perry's "Teenage Dream" album to reach #1 (tying the 1988 feat by Michael Jackson's "Bad") while the NBC TV musical competition "The Voice" fathered the year's strangest dance craze, "Moves Like Jagger" (Maroon 5 featuring Christina Aguilera) where dancers mimic the outrageous stage prancing of The Rolling Stone's Mick Jagger.

"Pumped Up Kicks" (Foster The People) rendered a sinister lyric of violent intent disguised by placid harmonies, whistling and a rollicking beat, while "The Lazy Song" (Bruno Mars) celebrated the joy of doing nothing and "Faster" (Matt Nathanson) borrowed from the time-honored rhythm of the 1955 standard "Bo Diddley". "Without You" (David Guetta featuring Usher) was merely a sampling from the album "Nothing But The Beat" which included Guetta's duets with other music luminaries including Jennifer Hudson, Timbaland, Nicki Ninaj and Chris Brown.

Artists entering new phases included Grace Potter And The Nocturnals, Rolling Stone Magazine's Best Rock Group of 2010, abandoning rock for country music, and REM retiring after a thirty-year career.

Additional highlights of 2011 included "Tonight Tonight" (Hot Chellie Rae), "You And I" (Lady Gaga), "If I Die Young" (The Band Perry) and "For The First Time" (The Script).

Seventy-eight-year-old Jerry Leiber whose songwriting collaborations with Mike Stoller shaped rock &

roll in its formative years died August 22 in Los Angeles.

2012

Billboard Magazine declared 2012 the year of the new artist with six of the top ten positions on the Year End Survey occupied by new acts including the top three: #1) "Somebody That I Used To Know" (Gotye featuring Kimbra), #2) "Call Me Maybe" (Carly Rae Jepsen), #3) "We Are Young" (Fun featuring Janelle Monae).

Another of those acts, the British boy band One Direction (that placed at #10 with "What Makes You Beautiful") went from appearances on the U.K. talent show *The X Factor* to having their first two albums "Up All Night" and "Take Me Home" enter The Billboard 200 at #1, the first group from England to do so.

The Grammy Awards on February 12 mixed triumph and tragedy. After scooping up all six awards for which she was nominated, Adele gave a bravura performance proving that her voice was back in full form following surgery. Her album "21" would be Billboard's Top Album for the second year in a row (the first time an album had reigned over two calendar years since Michael Jackson's "Thriller" during 1983/84). But a cloud hung over the proceedings with the death of Whitney Houston the day before from a combination of drugs and alcohol. Houston's funeral was televised nationally a week later.

The oddest social trend of the year, the video "Gangnam Style" (Psy) was the first in history to break the barrier of 1 billion views on YouTube. Psy (shorthand for psycho) invoked a cheesy horse riding dance in contrast to his classier fashion sense in this satire of the conspicuous consumption of the affluent Gangnam neighborhood of Seoul, South Korea.

Controversy continued to surround streaming services including Spotify, Rhapsody, Muve Music, Slacker and Sony Music Unlimited with artists including Rhianna, Taylor Swift and Coldplay withholding their song catalogs believing that availability there was hurting CD sales.

Several nationally televised concerts were staged to raise money for the victims of Hurricane Sandy featuring such acts as Bruce Springsteen, Billy Joel, Christina Aguilera and Paul McCartney. Katy Perry's concert tour came to theaters as the 3-D film "Part Of Me" while Madonna's MDNA tour kicked up a catfight by making a medley of "Express Yourself" with Lady Gaga's "Born This Way", implying that the latter borrowed too heavily from the former. The Rolling Stones also hit the road for a 50th anniversary concert tour.

The most severe concert moment came from Russia where the female punk rock group Pussy Riot received two-year prison sentences for performing songs in public that were unacceptable to the Putin administration. Public outcry against the injustice had no effect.

A frequently asked question of the year was why so many hit songs were appearing on radio and in video three months or more before the CD was available. "Brokenhearted" (Karmin), "Want U. Back" (Cher Lloyd) and "We Are Never Ever Getting Back Together" (Taylor Swift) were examples of songs that finally reached the record store long after radio was done with them.

Two vintage rock acts returned with their first albums in a decade – "Push And Shove" (No Doubt) and "That's Why God Made The Radio" (The Beach Boys). The latter demonstrated amazing vocal harmony from a group nearing the age of 70. It was also a year of sad goodbyes including the deaths of Dick Clark, Don Cornelius and Donna Summer.

The movie "Searching For Sugar Man" featured the year's least likely musical star, Sixto Rodriguez who recorded two commercially unsuccessful albums for Motown during the 1970s. One of those albums, "Cold Fact", was banned by the South African government for seditious undertones, the reason that a South African fan nicknamed The Sugar Man (after a Rodriguez song) launched a successful campaign to locate his forgotten idol over thirty years later.

2013

Like the music video of the same name in which she appeared nude Miley Cyrus came in like a "Wrecking Ball" pushing all of the hot buttons for controversy. Her performance at the MTV Video Music Awards featured her twerking in a flesh colored bikini while utilizing a stadium foam finger to simulate sex. She insulted "Today" show host Matt Lauer by telling him, "Oh, you're definitely not sexual", because he was 55 years old. She also appeared as a nymphomaniac takeoff of Congresswoman Michelle Bachman at a wildly permissive gathering of well-known Republicans in an over the top "Saturday Night Live" comedy sketch.

The purpose behind the craziness was to distance herself from that overly wholesome teen she portrayed on the Disney Channel series "Hannah Montana". Ironically, her album "Bangerez" received critical praise while its hits including "We Can't Stop" topped the chart before the nuttiness ever began. 2013 would go down as the year that everyone was talking about that wild child Miley Cyrus.

"Blurred Lines" (Robin Thicke featuring T.J. And Pharrell) attracted most of the year's musical heat. It was Billboard's #1 song for airplay, the top video of 2013 at VH1 and the subject of a social discussion with its contrast of the behavior of good girls and bad girls and whether or not the song was advocating rape. In a pre-emptive legal strike Thicke, T.J. And Pharrell filed a law suit against Marvin Gaye's family for claiming that "Blurred Lines" held more than a passing resemblance to Gaye's "Got To Give It Up". At year's end Pharrell Williams was reaching greater heights with "Happy" from the "Despicable Me 2" soundtrack with its infectiously upbeat video.

"Royals" (Lorde), a hit about materialistic rock stars who can't relate to the lives of normal people, supposedly originated when the 17-year old singing star from New Zealand was inspired by a picture of former Kansas City Royals baseball legend George Brett in a 1976 issue of National Geographic. All Lorde could remember was the Royals uniform. As farfetched as the story seemed Lorde collected old issues of National Geographic Magazine.

Self esteem songs including "Q.U.E.E.N." (Janelle Monae), "Treasure" (Bruno Mars), "Lighthouse" (Fantasia) and "Girl On Fire" (Alicia Keys) were supplementing the self-worth of listeners. In a more tightly focused sense "Same Love" (McLemore and Ryan Lewis) became an anthem for gay rights.

The year's top album "The 20/20 Experience" (Justin Timberlake) sold 968,000 copies its first week while "Unorthodox Jukebox" (Bruno Mars) cranked out a variety of #1 hits including "Locked Out Of Heaven" and "When I Was Your Man", earning him the honor to star in the 2014 Super Bowl halftime show where his dance moves reminded many of James Brown in his prime.

The year's eye-popping stage spectacle belonged to the concert tour by Pink mixing gymnastics, acrobatics, dance and aerial feats. Suspended by cables above the audience Pink performed her catalog of hits while soaring dangerously close to the chorus of audience cell phones snapping every picture of the action. A show in constant motion released as the DVD "The Truth About Love Tour".

Movies made a major impact on 2013. The documentary "One Direction: This Is Us" grossed $28.9 million, more than any other music movie that year. A second documentary "20 Feet From Stardom" trained the spotlight on the talented background singers whose voices have supported the biggest names in the music business. The hit "Cups" from the soundtrack to "Pitch Perfect" made an unexpected singing star of actress Anna Kendrick who utilized an infectious choreography involving cups in the music video.

In leftover business from 2012 Lady Gaga finally

answered Madonna's accusation that "Born This Way" had ripped off Madonna's 1989 hit "Express Yourself". During a comedy routine on "Saturday Night Live" about the world's worst cover records the title "Express Yourself" appeared on screen while Gaga burst forth with "Born This Way". Just back from hip surgery Lady Gaga had a busy year. Her music video "Applause" premiered her clam shell bikini, a bra with black hands and her angry rolling on the floor as if in seizures. Meanwhile her Born Brave Bus at concerts supported anti-bullying efforts, suicide prevention and mental health for young adults.

Other memorable moments for the year included the top hit in the Billboard Hot 100 for 2013 "Thrift Shop" (McLemore and Ryan Lewis); "Broadway Idiot", a Broadway musical based on the songs of Green Day; the music video "Brave" (Sarah Bareilles) giving everyone camera time who will perform a goofy dance; and the year's greatest misstep when fashion chain Abercrombie And Fitch was forced to pull its t-shirts reading "more boyfriends than t.s." after Taylor Swift fans flooded the company with complaints.

Members of the Russian rock group Pussy Riot were released from prison at year's end only to be brutally pummeled by clubs and whips at a public performance some weeks afterward for singing a song critical of Vladimar Putin.

2014

"Happy" (Pharrell Williams), Billboard's top hit for 2014, continued to resonate in various ways from Pharrell replacing Cee Lo Green as a judge on NBC TV's "The Voice" to the arrest in Iran of a group calling itself "The Happy In Teheran Dancers" who showed their dance moves in a widely circulated video. The Iranian government sentenced the dancers to 91 lashes and six months in prison for cavorting in public, eventually suspending the sentences.

Taylor Swift's album "1989" abandoned country for pop at the same time that she pulled her music from the sharing site Spotify. "Music is art and art is important and rare", Swift declared. "Important things in life are valuable. Valuable things should be paid for." Whether her one woman crusade could slow the erosion of record sales would require time to confirm.

"All About The Bass" (Meghan Trainor) was the year's serious statement regarding body image although the song was encased in an infectious radio hook. "Problem" and "Fancy" both by Australian rapper Iggy Azelea crowned the teenage talent as a style setter for American teens.

The video sharing site Vimeo opened a new direction in music with Kawehi's cover of Nirvana's "Heart Shaped Box". The song employed "looping", a process where a tune is deconstructed, separating each componant such as bass, drums and vocal, then piecing it back together with original material inserted by the artist. Both Esquire and The Huffington Post printed rave reviews of Kawehi's video.

Controversies during the year included Katy Perry's "Dark Horse" video which was forced to delete a scene of a man wearing an "Allah" necklace before turning into dust. A petition with 65,000 signatures claimed that using the word in this way was blasphemous.

Miley Cyrus again proved to be a magnet of controversy after being banned from performing in The Dominican Republic. A government commission claimed that she "undertakes acts that go against morals and customs that are punishable by Dominican law." A September 13 concert in Santo Domingo was cancelled. Meanwhile in the U.S. the photo featuring Miley's pet pig Bubba Sue with a pedicure received complaints from animal activists. To her credit Miley utlized her appearance at the MTV Video Music Awards to announce her efforts to raise money for charities addressing teen homelessness.

It was not a good year for Bono of U2 who broke his hand, shoulder, elbow and bones in his face during a biking accident. The band went on the road with replacement singers including Bruce Springsteen while Bono announced that he may never be capable of playing the guitar again.

Retro currents continued to flood music. The "Girls Chase Boys" music video by Ingrid Michaelson provided gender reversal from Robert Palmer's 1980s videos, this time with "robot men" instead of women. Mark Ronson and Bruno Mars recreated 70s style soul music with "Uptown Funk".

The albums "The Endless River" (Pink Floyd), "Queen Forever" (Queen) and "Xscape" (Micheal Jackson) updated unreleased archival material while the movie "Get On Up" starred Chadwick Boseman as the 1960s godfather of soul James Brown. After more than a year of public confrontation between his wife and daughter deceased radio legend Casey Kasem was finally buried in December.

The National Football League briefly floated the unpopular idea of requiring musical performers to pay for the privelege of headlining The Super Bowl halftime show before signing Katy Perry to do it in 2015 at no personal expense.

On a lighter note the music video "Ain't It Fun" (Paramore) set the most world records in a video with such unusual achievements as the most vinyl records smashed in a minute and the quickest run backward blindfolded for thirty feet while holding stuffed animals.

* * *

The book ends here, but the music doesn't. Too many before me have stated it more passionately... "You can't stop rock and roll." "Rock and roll is here to stay." "It will stand."

The will always be a teenage singer pleading to be understood by the adult world, a bubblegum teen idol contrasted to a more threatening guitar player attempting to melt your amps, an R&B singer pouring it out from his/her soul and thumping, throbbing dance beat that can't be resisted. These roles repeat throughout the history of the music and will continue to do so.

Each generation will rephrase these themes achieving a temporary immortality until the next generation throws it all out and starts over again. Billy Murray was the record industry's first pop star during the early years of the

20th century, yet 100 years later he is almost totally forgotten by the popular culture that he fathered during its formative years except for devoted historians who keep the interest alive in his songs of World War I, the Women's Suffrage Movement and early 20th century industrialization.

Like the other music, this could be rock and roll's eventual fate. One hundred years from now it will relate its story of these times. If they listen.

APPENDIX 1

10 BONA FIDE ONE-HIT WONDERS

1)   SH-BOOM, The Chords (1954) A textbook example of what went wrong during the 1950s . The Chords, a black group, wrote "Sh-Boom" and made the original recording, but a white pop group, The Crew Cuts, rushed out a cover record that actually beat the original to the Chart and soaked up all the pop glory. Many pop stations refused to air black artists, giving The Crew Cuts an advantage over The Chords. The Crew Cuts went on to have a series of hits, many of them covers, while The Chords vanished as quickly as they appeared.

2)   A LITTLE BIT OF SOAP, The Jarmels (1961) Sampling is nothing new. This hit owed its success to that musical snippet of Ben E. King's "Stand By Me" which was instrumentally inserted. Any song that could bank off an existing hit was assured some degree of commercial success.

3)   POPSICLES AND ICICLES, The Murmaids (1963) The song's author was David Gates who would lead the 70s group Bread, the producer Kim Fowley who also found fame in the 70s producing The Runaways. This would be the only hit for both The Murmaids and their label, Chattahoochie Records. The girls concentrated on their college studies

instead of hitting the road to promote this song which made it to #3 Pop. The arrival of The Beatles at year's end abbreviated the careers of many acts atop the Chart.

4) FARMER JOHN, The Premiers (1964) They were a pioneering Chicano band, but their vocal sounded like a black group. The women of the Corvalis Car Club were brought in to scream their lungs out in an attempt to out-Beatle the Beatles. The noisy record found its place, but the group couldn't come up with another gimmick for a sequel.

5) IN THE SUMMERTIME, Mungo Jerry (1970) Frequently a one-hit act in America has a full-blown music career in another region of the world. Dave, Dee, Dozy, Beaky, Mick and Tich had a series of innovative hits in their native England, yet only placed one hit on the U.S. charts – "Hold Tight" (1966), while Norway's "a-ha" was one of the enduring European bands of the 1980s even though their sole chart entry in the U.S. was "Take On Me" (1986). Another English act, Mungo Jerry, found fame with "In The Summertime" both in England and the U.S. They had a series of hits in England, but in the states this was their lone Chart accomplishment, a hit with an unexpected Caribbean feel.

6) GOOD TIME CHARLIE'S GOT THE BLUES, Danny O'Keefe (1972) This hit for all the hippies burnt out on drugs and free love was a reality check for the 70s with its lesson in mortality. Danny O'Keefe continued recording critically acclaimed

albums through the 1990s including "Breezy Stories" and "So Long Harry Truman", but the commercial buck and hits stopped here.

7) KISS IN THE DARK, Pink Lady (1979) The most classic case of bad timing. Pink Lady sold 100 million records in their native Japan, but they tried to storm America at the moment that national anger was boiling over the trade imbalance between the U.S. and Japan (particularly automobiles) and just as disco, the underpinning of their music, was dying. "Kiss In The Dark" spent two weeks in the Top Forty during 1979, while the duo's 1980 NBC TV series "Pink Lady And Jeff" lasted only six episodes.

8) GENIUS OF LOVE, Tom Tom Club (1982) Moonlighting from their regular roles in the art/rock group The Talking Heads, Tina Weymouth and her husband, Chris Frantz, created this futuristic music arrangement that would return in subsequent hits by Mariah Carey and Tupac Shakur. A very influential performance that is still being felt today.

9) JUMP AROUND, House Of Pain (1992) A white group rapping for Irish pride and a tribute to the dance, The Pogo. Many white rappers like Vanilla Ice and Snow were deemed posers, but this hit was the real deal, a true rap standard that was inescapable in its many applications in movies and television. Everlast emerged from the group, but they never found a sequel for this pervasive hit.

10) THAT THING YOU DO!, The Wonders (1996) Five actors with no musical ability were transformed into

a functional rock band for Tom Hank's 1996 film about the divisions that tear a fictitious group apart in 1964 after their only hit. In a case of life imitating art, the group's follow-up, "Little Wild One", went nowhere, making The Wonders the film embodiment of the one-hit wonder.

APPENDIX 2

THE TOP TEN THAT NEVER WERE

1)   A tape, possibly three-hours long, of an impromptu jam session between Elvis Presley and The Beatles which occurred at Presley's Bel-Air mansion on August 27, 1965. Its whereabouts unknown, the tape would represent the only occasion that these two giants performed together.

2)   The dirty version of "Louie Louie" by The Kingsmen (1963) College students in both Indiana and Ohio surfaced with the dirty lyrics of the song when spun at a slower speed. But after a year-and-a-half investigation by the FBI, no definitive conclusion was reached.

3)   "From A Window" recorded by The Beatles during a 1962 radio broadcast in England. One of their last remaining rarities that hasn't appeared on record (except for a version by Billy J. Kramer).

4)   "Love Me Tender" by Elvis Presley and Linda Ronstadt (1977)

5)   "We're All Alone" by Boz Scaggs and Rita Coolidge (1978) Two performances spliced together by a disc jockey and distributed to radio stations nationwide. Neither duo ever recorded together and the tapes were never released on record.

6) "Mrs. O'Leary's Cow" by The Beach Boys (1966) After a fire broke out in the recording studio next to the one where this song was recorded, the group considered it a bad omen and destroyed the only tape of this song about the great Chicago fire complete with the sound of sirens and flames crackling. Brian Wilson re-recorded the song from memory for his 2004 album "Smile."

7) "Claudine" by The Rolling Stones (1980) To prevent a possible lawsuit, Atlantic Records deleted this song about the shooting of pro skier Spider Sabich from the "Emotional Rescue" LP.

8) 80 songs recorded but not released for the "Music Of My Mind" LP by Stevie Wonder (1972). Stevie said they weren't ready.

9) Led Zeppelin's last tracks, 1980, for an album left unfinished in the wake of drummer John Bonham's death.

10) The greatest non-gathering of talent during the 1980s—the acts that didn't sing on "We Are The World": Prince (he was invited but didn't attend), Janet Jackson (the only member of the family not present), Madonna, John Cougar, Joan Jett, Heart, The Eurythmics, Genesis, Pat Benetar, Z Z Top, The Rolling Stones, and George Thorogood.

APPENDIX 3

ROCK & ROLL CHRISTMAS

1) ELVIS' CHRISTMAS ALBUM (1957) Apart from a few R&B singles for the holidays, rock & roll really didn't make a major push into the genre until "Elvis' Christmas Album" which debuted December 2, 1957 on the Billboard Album Chart, eventually reaching #1. The album had no singles hit, but radio played Elvis' remake of the 1950 Ernest Tubb country hit "Blue Christmas" as if it were a single. The album was an odd mix of gospel, rock and provincial fare. Teenagers were ecstatic, stodgier quarters appalled. It opened the door for hits such as "Jingle Bell Rock" (Bobby Helms) and "Merry Christmas" (The Cameos), both 1957 and "Rockin' Around The Christmas Tree" (Brenda Lee) and "Run Rudolph Run" (Chuck Berry), both 1958. Christmas music would never be the same.

2) A CHRISTMAS GIFT FOR YOU FROM PHILLIES RECORDS (1963) Released on November 22, 1963 (the day JFK was killed), this album featured Phil Spector's patented wall-of-sound arrangements of well-known Christmas songs by The Ronettes, The Crystals, Darlene Love and Bob B. Soxx & The Blue Jeans. Those arrangements were mimicked decades later on Christmas albums by Mariah Carey and Hilary Duff, while The Crystals' performance of "Santa Claus Is Coming To Town" with its subtle modification to

the chorus became the blueprint for all future versions of the song including those by The Jackson Five, Bruce Springsteen and The Pointer Sisters.

3)   AMEN, The Impressions (1964) Written by Jester Hairston, the former director of The Hall Johnson Choir during the 1930s, "Amen" first came to the attention of the public in the 1963 Sidney Poitier film "Lillies Of The Field". The following year, Curtis Mayfield & The Impressions took the song to #7 Pop at Christmastime in deference to that year's trend toward English Invasion and Motown. The song spread to black church services and even became an anthem of the Civil Rights Movement.

4)   SOMEDAY AT CHRISTMAS, Stevie Wonder (1966) This wasn't your parent's feel good Christmas hit. "Someday At Christmas" held up a mirror to all that was wrong with the world—war, tyranny, weapons of mass destruction—to remind us that we're falling short of the Christmas ideal. As the first Christmas hit with a social conscience, it reached #24 on the Billboard Christmas Chart in 1966.

5)   THIS CHRISTMAS, Donny Hathaway (1970) Simply a song about a man and a woman sharing intimacy during the holidays, "This Christmas" was underappreciated at first, spending only one week on the Billboard Christmas Chart in 1972 at #11. During the next thirty years, nearly every major soul act recorded it including The Temptations, The Whispers, The Jets, Patti Labelle, Usher, Freddy Jackson, All-4-One, Dru Hill, SWV, Etta James,

Jeffrey Osborne, Destiny's Child and Ashanti making it the most widely recorded soul Christmas classic.

6) FELIZ NAVIDAD, Jose Feliciano (1970) The Latino Christmas hit even with Spanish lyrics and title. It finally reached the Billboard Pop Chart in 1998, peaking at #70.

7) LITTLE DRUMMER BOY/PEACE ON EARTH, Bing Crosby & David Bowie (1977/1995) Originally a segment from Bing Crosby's last CBS Christmas Special in 1977, this odd moment in Christmas music paired a toned down Bowie with one of the leading singers from the 1920s-40s. And a moment of magic happened between the two generations. Years later, MTV brought the film out of mothballs and started airing it as a holiday music video. VH-1 followed suit and repeated airings resulted in the performance being released as a CD single in 1993. It peaked at #43 on the Billboard Pop Chart in 2002.

8) DO THEY KNOW IT'S CHRISTMAS?, Band-Aid (1984) Raising $11 million to combat the Ethiopian famine, this hit put Christmas idealism into practice while spanning a worldwide philanthropy movement in music during the 80s. A 20th anniversary re-recording of the song by Band Aid 20 in 2004 continued the legacy for the same cause.

9) A VERY SPECIAL CHRISTMAS (1987) This album series to benefit Special Olympics made its bow in 1987 and has featured memorable cuts by Madonna, The Eurythmics, Vanessa Williams, Jon

Bon Jovi, John Mellancamp and others.

10)   PLATINUM CHRISTMAS (2000) This album
       moved Christmas music into the 21st century with
       contemporary material performed by Britney Spears,
       The Backstreet Boys, N'Sync, Christina Aguilera,
       Joe, TLC and others. Britney's track "My Only Wish
       (This Year)" appeared on two other compilation
       albums within two years, the mark of a new classic.

Made in the USA
Lexington, KY
29 July 2017